# A FLAVOR OF
# TUSCANY

# A Flavor of
# TUSCANY

## VIVIENNE GONLEY

ILLUSTRATIONS BY PAUL COLLICUTT

CHARTWELL
BOOKS, INC.

Massa

Lucca

Pisa

Bologna

R. Arno  Firenze

Volterra

Livorno

Siena

Piombino

R. Ombrone

Grosseto

N

Roma

A sk an Italian countryman to define Italian food and your question will be met with a puzzled shrug – "La cucina *italiana*? behh . . ." Differences between Ligurian, Lombardian, Piedmontese, Napolitan, Sicilian or Emilian food will be painstakingly and lovingly explained, conversation invariably developing into debate as others are drawn in. From the snow-clad Alps on the Austrian border to the sweltering plains of Calábria, Italy is a country of contrasts. History and geography have conspired to make each region what it is. Food, elevated to an almost religious status in Italy, is the strongest statement of a region's identity. People are even defined by what they eat – Napolitans are known as *mangiamaccheroni* (pasta-eaters) and Tuscans *mangiofagioli* (bean-eaters).

# INTRODUCTION

Differences in cuisine are still the hallmark of each region. In Naples, for example, the thin, uneven pizza cooked in a wood oven has evolved from a cheap street-snack into an art form. Toppings for soft breads and pasta sauces make imaginative use of plum tomatoes, huge and sweet from the southern sun. Here too, *mozzarella di bufala* (buffalo-milk mozzarella) from the herds that have been raised since Roman times, is prized. With its soft texture and distinctive flavor it is eaten on its own, with just a little salt and olive oil. Sicily, being surrounded by water, offers both exceptional seafood and, a relic of centuries of Moorish domination, exquisite cakes of almonds and orange blossom. The North's cooler climate allows for cattle-rearing for Lombardy's creamy risotto and Emilia-Romagna's Gorgonzola and Parmesan cheeses.

And Bologna is known as *la grassa* – the fatty – because of its dedication to the pleasures of the table. Its streets are full of food shops whose windows are piled high with

*mortadella* ham, wheels of Parmesan and bulging *tortellini*.

Italians are convinced that the basis of good eating lies in quality seasonal ingredients. Nowhere is this more true than in lush, green Tuscany, whose temperate climate, fertile soil and brilliant light make it possible to produce a wide variety of crops around the year. This is a region of small hill farms, punctuated by cypress trees and patchwork fields; of long vistas and gently undulating hills, silvery olive groves and orderly vineyards; of pastel-colored medieval hilltop towns, evocative of the frescos of Filippo Lippi and Piero della Francesca. Tuscany is heart-shaped and lies in the center of Italy. The Ligurian Sea flanks the West, the lushly fertile Mugello region and spectacular Apuan Alps lie in the North. To the East is the wooded Arezzo valley where the river Arno meets the Chiana. On either side of the southernmost tip lie the great ridge of Monte Amiata and the forests of the Maremma. In the middle lie Florence, Siena and the medieval hilltop towns – the small region people think of as classic Tuscany.

With its profusion of rivers, valleys, coastline and mountains, together with so many surrounding neighbors in the regions of Emilia-Romagna, Liguria, Le Marche and Umbria, it is not surprising that Tuscan cooking is so diverse. Robust wild boar dishes from the Maremma contrast markedly with richer, creamier dishes of the

San Gimignano – one of Tuscany's many magical hilltop towns.

a type of cooking, known as *cucina povera* – the country cooking of the peasants – gradually evolved.

Despite the name, the *cucina povera* wasn't reserved for the peasants. From the eighth century until the 1960's, when mechanization took over, the land in Tuscany was worked by a system called *mezzadria* (from *a mezzo*, "half and half"), by which profits were shared between landowner and worker. The system made for an equality of sorts between master and farm workers, at least in food terms, since the landowners were frugal and on the whole favored the simple produce of their own land. Apart from game, which was strictly reserved for the landlord, everybody on the *mezzadria* ate the same things. Almost austere in its simplicity, *cucina povera* relies on the raw ingredients as the main determinant of a dish's success. And, thanks to a blessed climate and thrifty use of the land, there were always good basics to work with. Simple, unfussy food was created from the best of the season's crops with minimum adornment, allowing the flavors to speak for themselves. Tuscans knew too well that, as the saying goes, "You can't make a silk purse out of a sow's ear."

Based on centuries-old rhythms of the land, the dishes have changed little today, with the commitment to using prime quality ingredients as strong as ever. A hearty *minestra* soup made with the season's best vegetables, a dish of wild asparagus dressed with unfiltered olive oil, or a tender Florentine steak grilled simply over embers are prime examples of unfussy Tuscan fare. This book aims to bring alive Tuscany's unadulterated flavors and help you bring simple cooking to your own table, through confident use of minimum basic ingredients.

Mugello or the delectable Umbrian-inspired truffle dishes found in southeastern Tuscany.

## CUCINA POVERA

Typical Tuscan food is, and has always been, country food. Walking through the medieval city gates, Tuscans for centuries found themselves in the midst of open countryside and surrounded by wheat fields, olive groves and vineyards. Merchants and landowners lived in the town, but had regular dealings with the countryside. Constant movement between town and country ensured the link between what grew on the land and what people ate. Thus,

*The massive fortress at Montalcino, a solid reminder of Tuscany's often war-torn past.*

### CUCINA ALTA-BORGHESE

While peasant and landowner lived off the *cucina povera*, there was another strain of cooking, known as *cucina alta-borghese*, which developed among the nobility. The aristocracy were well traveled and therefore had constant access to new ingredients and ideas. Their cooking, inventive and often ostentatious, flourished during the Renaissance when Florence was the cultural hub of Europe.

The Renaissance social scene revolved around the banquet – a time to show off, to see and be seen – and hosts would try to outdo each other in ever more elaborate dishes. Armies of cooks would be exhorted to prepare complicated game and boar dishes, stiff, savory jellies, stuffed meats and sculptures of sugar to decorate the tables.

To bypass the sumptuary laws of the time, which forbade more than three courses at one sitting, cooks had to be artful. Many different, and often unlikely, ingredients would be combined into one dish. One over-zealous cook suggested stuffing a wild boar with a pig, with a lamb with a chicken with a quail with a thrush!

The Italian courts also led the way in table etiquette. The diaries of an English sixteenth-century traveler recorded ". . . a custom . . . not used in any other country that I saw in my travels. The Italians do always at their meals use a little fork when they cut the meat . . ." Part of Tuscany's proud folklore is that it passed on these manners and certain dishes to France, when Catherine de' Medici married a French prince in 1535. Arriving in France with her retinue of cooks, she is said to have inspired certain French classic dishes, such as onion soup, duck with orange sauce and pork with prunes.

In the sixteenth century, the spice trade with the East was still flourishing, bringing saffron, ginger, cinnamon, cloves, nutmeg and pepper into the Renaissance kitchen. Thought of as both exotic and wholesome, spices were used as stimulants – these were the days before tea and coffee – and to disguise the taste of imperfectly cured meat or fish. Medicinally, saffron was prescribed for anything from bloodshot eyes to damaged hair, nutmeg for chest complaints, and cinnamon for problems of the liver.

Cloves, nutmeg and cinnamon gave distinct flavors to sweetmeats, such as the nutty, spicy *panforte* and *panpepato*, while ginger was used in jellies and jams and saffron to color sauces yellow. *Agrodolce* (sour-sweet) dishes, in which meat and game were

*The fabled bounty of the Tuscan vineyards.*

combined with fruit and spices, were popular too. Many of these dishes are eaten in Tuscany today, showing that the influence of the Renaissance lives on. *Cinghiale in agrodolce* (wild boar with chocolate and pine nuts) *faraona alla Medici* (guinea fowl with prunes) *cipolline in agrodolce* (little sweet onions) and the fruit and spice cake *panforte di Siena* are to be found on Tuscan tables and their recipes are included in this book.

### PATTERNS OF THE YEAR

The *cucina povera* was, above all, seasonal. The labors of the land were clearly marked out from January to December, the right time for sowing and reaping often being determined by lunar rhythms. After each harvest, the produce was distributed through the *mezzadria*, while the

rest was carefully preserved and stored to vary the diet throughout the rest of the year.

Old harvest traditions are still very much alive in Tuscany. The country year is punctuated by *sagre*, village fairs which mark a particular harvest or food with open-air dinners for the villagers and their guests. Like all Italians, Tuscans love to celebrate. There are *sagre* for pine nuts, in the tiny village of Chiesanuova near Florence, for *cacciucco* fish soup in Livorno, for beef in Cortona, for *pecorino* cheese in Pienza, for wild mushrooms around Monte Amiata, for Chianti and *schiacciata all'uva* (flat grape bread) in Greve, for wild boar in Capalbio and for chestnut flour in Marradi.

The rhythm of the agricultural year has remained largely unchanged over the centuries. It starts with the slaughtering of the pig – a tradition dating back to Roman times when

Ancient olive trees are a well-loved part of the Italian landscape.

this sacrifice was made to will the land's fertility. The following weeks are taken up with using every part of the animal wisely: the curing of the ham for *prosciutto* and the making of *salami*, sausages and other sustaining dishes to see through the winter months. *Porchetta* (suckling pig) and *arrista di maiale* (roast loin of pork with rosemary and garlic) appear at market stalls.

*Pecorino* cheese-making begins in March, when the lambs are sufficiently weaned for the ewes' milk curds to be used for slow-maturing cheese and the whey for making wobbly ricotta. In spring, the olive trees are pruned, in good time for the harvest later in the year. Fava beans, asparagus and artichokes are picked and eaten with the previous year's olive oil. In June, the *cannellini* and *borlotti* bean crop, one of the biggest and most important, is harvested, to be enjoyed for the rest of the year in simple salads with onion and olive oil and in soups.

In the heat of July, the corn fields are reaped, and harvest celebrations follow. The vine tomatoes of late summer are eaten on grilled country bread as *bruschetta* and in tomato and bread salad – *panzanella* – or with *pisci*, "poor man's" pasta. Autumn's *porcini* mushrooms, gathered from the woods in huge basketfuls, are eaten with garlic and parsley, chopped into soups and risottos, or dried as *porcini*

*secchi*. Late autumn brings the harvest of Tuscany's two most important crops, olives and vines. And at the end of the year, walnuts, almonds and hazelnuts are gathered and made into *panforte*, the rich nougat made with honey to bring with it a rich and sweet new year. Lentils – symbolizing the seeds to be planted – are eaten on New Year's Eve in a centuries-old tradition of encouraging the land's fertility for the coming year. Tuscan cuisine has deviated so little from the rhythms of the land that country people still think of the year in terms of crops, rather than months.

THE OLIVE HARVEST

The simplicity and grace of Tuscan cooking relies on using prime olive oil, and Tuscany produces arguably the best in Italy. Used as much raw as it is for cooking, its vintage and provenance are taken very seriously. Most households keep a bottle of the best green, unfiltered oil to drizzle over leaf salads, steaks, country bread and freshly cooked vegetables.

Then they will have a large quantity of cooking oil of less exceptional pedigree at hand. The small town of Lucca has always laid claim to producing the best oil, a claim which has of course been hotly disputed by its Tuscan competitors in the surrounding towns and villages.

Terrible frosts in 1985 killed almost half the olive trees in Tuscany, some of which were six hundred years old, decreasing output and making the price rocket. The large producers were obliged to blend their oil with cheaper oils from the South and southern Spain. Where the roots of the ancient trees were found to have survived, new trees were planted in old trunks.

The oil is bright green, fruity and peppery with a sharp piquancy when newly made. Its character derives from a combination of factors: soil type, climate, positioning of the groves on slopes so that the olives get the full impact of the sun, and, of course, the craftsmanship of knowing just when to prune and when to gather.

Late November, when the olives are purple and not fully ripe, is harvest time. The community's men climb ladders and gather the olives by hand, while the women pick the freshly fallen olives from the ground. Tuscans have learned from centuries of oil-making that gentle treatment of the

olive tree pays off in a greater yield. Older Tuscans are so practiced at the arduous job of hand-picking that they are said to be able to gather over 200 pounds in a day!

At the local press – often an ancient stone mill where olives have been crushed for centuries – they are made into oil. Throughout Tuscany, there are *aziende olearie*, co-operatives of small producers whose yield is not enough to produce their own vintage and who combine their oil with that of their neighbors for commercial purposes.

The first drops of rich, deep green oil which run out from the first pressing, known as *olio di prima spremitura* (first pressed), is the very best. It is clear if filtered, cloudy if left unfiltered. At this point, *bruschetta* is eaten – the oil is drizzled onto country bread cooked over an open fire, to taste and celebrate the yield.

For the second quality of oil, virgin olive oil, the pulp still in the press is treated with heat and pressed a second time. This oil, paler, clearer and thinner with its less dominant taste and higher tolerance of heat, will be used for cooking and frying.

### HOW TO USE THE RECIPES

For Italians, the first stage of cooking – procuring the right ingredients – is often treated as the most important. Choosing a sleek, shiny fish, a tender slice of beef, a handful of sweet dark cherries, a perfectly ripe pear or some soft *prosciutto* to eat with small ripe figs is a skill which requires good judgement and a trained eye.

On market days, prodding, smelling, squeezing and sometimes lengthy discussion precede the final choosing. Stall holders, proud of their produce, give only the best. Packaging is done with love and care; a bag of ripe peaches will be puffed up with air to prevent the fruit bruising before arriving at the table. All this, of course, takes time, and a good dose of *pazienza* – patience – is required. Favorite dishes will be freely adapted to suit the best of the seasonal produce chosen on the day.

*Tuscany's restaurants are a point of pride for owners and customers alike.*

Most of the dishes in these pages have been handed down through the generations, by a tradition largely oblivious to written recipes. Italians have always tended to cook by intuition and experience, rather than by formula. It is hard to pin down an Italian country cook to an exact measurement – you will always be told, with a shrug, to use *un'etto* (about a quarter pound) or *una manciata* (a handful). This flexibility has come about through constantly adapting the dishes and their proportions to what is both available and good at any given time of the year.

Back in 1963, Elizabeth David talked about the necessity of adapting recipes to suit available ingredients in the introduction to her book *Italian Food*. At the time, parsley was often the only fresh herb to be found and fresh plum tomatoes unheard of. Thirty years later, things have changed. Global produce appears on our supermarket shelves all year round. Grown in greenhouse conditions, treated for a long shelf-life and wrapped in plastic, over-fat asparagus, insipid strawberries, woolly peaches and apricots lack flavor. The Italian attitude towards food – discernment in choosing ingredients and flexibility towards recipes – seems a good one to adopt, now more than ever.

Find good greengrocers, butchers and fishmongers and ask them what's tasty, local and seasonal. Buy whatever looks the best and, if necessary, adapt the recipe accordingly – this is, after all, the principle of rustic cooking. In the winter, for example, use potatoes for the *sformato*, instead of zucchini, and spinach or savoy cabbage for the stuffed crêpes, instead of asparagus. In spring, add some fava beans to the *minestrone* or use asparagus instead of tomatoes for a risotto. In summer serve *prosciutto* with small, sweet melon,

instead of figs. Once you have tried these recipes with the quantities and ingredients indicated, I hope you will use the book as a starting point for some inspired experimentation with seasonal ingredients, wherever you live. *Buon appetito!*

Whereas in the North of Italy the traditional staple is rice or polenta, in the South it is pasta and in the center it is bread. In Lorenzetti's fourteenth-century frescos on the walls of Siena's Palazzo Pubblico, the Sienese countryside in peace time depicts hillsides and flatlands given to the production of the biblical crops wheat, oil and vines, the food of all Mediterranean peoples and the consistent staples of the Tuscan diet.

Everyday Tuscan bread is called *pane di campagna* "country bread." It is light and open-textured. As the Tuscans say *cacio serrato e pane bucarellato* "tight-textured cheese and open-textured bread." As the main component of the peasants' diet, it was made with coarsely ground flour – that for the landowners would have been made with more refined flour – and with no salt, since in medieval times a tax was levied on salt. The practice of omitting salt has continued, and is not without its

# BREADS, BEANS AND PASTA

advantages. Tuscans insist that a saltless bread will show off the highly seasoned flavors of the locally cured hams and sheep's cheeses. Lack of salt does make the bread dry up quickly and, since the Tuscans are a frugal lot, a whole host of recipes designed to use up the previous day's bread has evolved. Bread will appear, grilled and drizzled with olive oil, underneath soup, or broken up into the soup itself for a *ribollita* or vegetable *minestra di verdura*. In summer, it forms the basis of the famous tomato salad *panzanella*. *Pane di campagna* is grilled over the fire and drizzled with olive oil for *bruschetta*. And for appetizers, little pieces of bread are toasted to make *crostini*, with delicious toppings of chicken livers, mushrooms and truffles, or puréed artichokes.

For these recipes, if you are lucky enough to have a good Italian baker near you, use one of their rustic breads, one to two days old. If not, a coarse white bread such as *ciabatta*, or a day-old French baguette, would do fine.

Other breads eaten in Tuscany are *foccaccia*, a flat, salty olive oil bread, and *schiacciata*, which literally means "squashed," due to its flat, uneven shape – a bread studded with grapes during the autumn grape harvest and with olives and rosemary during the olive harvest. *Ciabatta*, eaten throughout Italy, is a lighter olive-oil bread. The other type of bread found in every Tuscan town's bakery is *pane integrale*, a dark, nutty whole wheat bread.

### BEANS

Beans have been eaten in Italy since Roman times. In the Middle Ages, they were so valued that they were accepted as currency in the payment of taxes. In Tuscany, beans – *fagioli* – are so adored that, when, in times of regional feuds, detractors couldn't think of anything worse, they named the Tuscans *mangiafagioli* or bean-eaters. In the spring, tender sweet fava beans – *fave* – are eaten straight from their pods like fruit. After market days, you see the discarded pods, like banana skins, on the streets. These *fave* make a delicious starter with fresh sheep's-milk cheese and olive oil. In the summer, the white *cannellini* and the beautiful brown, speckled *borlotti* beans are harvested and dried in

quantity to last through the year. They are used to make the Tuscans' favorite side dish, *fagioli bianchi*, dressed with the purest olive oil and some wild sage leaves – or with tuna and capers – *zuppa di fagioli* – bean soup, or *fagioli all'uccelletto* where they are stewed in tomato sauce.

Small brown lentils – *lenticchie* – growing on the eastern borders of Tuscany and on the highland plains of neighboring Umbria are used to make wholesome soups or are stewed in a rich tomato sauce – *in umido* – with pure pork sausages. Chick-peas – *ceci* – boiled with a little rosemary, garlic and the greenest olive oil make a thick, peasanty soup.

### PASTA

Pasta has been a popular staple in Tuscany too. Homemade pastas typical of the region are *pappardelle*, wide noodles with a ruffled edge, traditionally served *all lepre* – with hare sauce, *tagliatelle* and *pisci* – which in Tuscan dialect mean "little strings." *Pisci* were originally served to celebrate the summer wheat harvest, accompanied with a rich sauce of duck – *anatra* – or goose – *oca*.

For special occasions, Tuscans make stuffed pasta. *Ravioli* are the favorite, stuffed with spinach and ricotta and dressed with butter and wild sage, or with a sauce of ground walnuts. In winter, pasta is often replaced with *gnocchi di patate* – little dumplings made from the season's floury white potatoes, in the Roman manner.

*The wheat harvest:*
*large bails of straw glow*
*in the warmth of the*
*late summer sun.*

# BRUSCHETTA

### TOASTED COUNTRY BREAD WITH OLIVE OIL

*In November the new oil from the olive harvest is celebrated in Tuscan and Umbrian villages with the making of* bruschetta. *This is the classic recipe, but many people add chopped tomato and basil, or finely sliced red onion and anchovies.*

#### SERVES 4

8 thick slices of coarse white bread, such as *ciabatta*
1 unpeeled garlic clove, cut in two

Cloudy green extra-virgin olive oil
Coarse sea salt

1 Toast the bread on a charcoal grill or under a broiler until it is very brown.

2 Rub each slice of bread on one side with the garlic and then drizzle over some olive oil and salt. Serve immediately. Bruschetta is usually eaten as an antipasto but it is also good as an accompaniment to salads.

# Schiacciata all'Uva

## FLORENTINE FLAT BREAD WITH BLACK GRAPES

*This delicious flat bread (schiacciata means "squashed") is made during
the October grape harvest and eaten outdoors at long tables for harvest lunches.
Tuscans often leave the seeds in, which gives the bread a strange crunch!*

### SERVES 8

FOR THE DOUGH
1½ ounces fresh cake yeast
1½ cups tepid water
1½ pounds (about 5 cups)
bread flour
Pinch of salt
½ cup sugar

FOR THE FILLING
1 pound black grapes, halved
and seeded
6 tablespoons sugar
A little beaten egg

1 Crumble the yeast and mix it with half the tepid water.

2 Sift the flour, salt and sugar into a bowl. Make a well in the center and pour in the yeast mixture and the rest of the water. Knead by hand, or in a mixer with a dough hook, for 5 minutes, until you have a soft, elastic dough.

3 Cover with a damp cloth and leave in a warm place for an hour, or until the dough has doubled in volume.

4 Knead again for 2–3 minutes. Divide the dough in two and roll each piece to fit a baking tray about 8 × 12 inches. Grease the baking tray and then cover it with one half of the rolled-out dough, scatter over half the grapes and half the sugar, and place the second piece on top. Seal the edges with your fingers.

5 Brush the top with beaten egg, push in the remaining grapes and sprinkle over the remaining sugar.

6 Leave in a warm place until the dough has doubled in volume again (about 20 minutes). Preheat the oven to 400°F.

7 Bake at the top of the oven for 40 minutes until the top is golden brown and the bottom sounds hollow when tapped. Cool on a wire rack.

*The grape harvest is a symbol of the bounty of late summer.*

19

# PANZANELLA

## SUMMER SALAD

*In Tuscan farmhouses,* panzanella *is made at the end of summer to use up gluts of tomatoes, red onions, cucumber and basil. The coarse, unsalted country bread (*pane di campagna*) dries up quickly, so this is also a good way of putting it to use.*

### SERVES 5–6

1 loaf of coarse white bread, such as baguette or *ciabatta*, 3–4 days old
6 large, over-ripe tomatoes, roughly chopped
1 large red onion, chopped
1 cucumber, diced
¼ cup pitted black olives, halved (optional)

4 tablespoons capers, drained and rinsed
Large handful of basil leaves, torn into shreds
Extra-virgin olive oil
Wine vinegar
Sea salt and freshly ground black pepper

1 Cut the bread into chunks and place them in a large bowl. Add the chopped tomatoes, onion and cucumber.

2 Toss the mixture together with salad servers and then stir in the olives (if using), capers and torn basil leaves.

3 Dress with a generous amount of good olive oil, a few drops of wine vinegar and plenty of salt and pepper. Mix well and refrigerate for one hour.

4 Toss the salad again to ensure there are no dry bread chunks. Leave in the refrigerator for another hour, or until the bread has absorbed all the juice, then adjust the seasoning and serve.

## Cook's Notes

Really stale, non-doughy bread is essential for this recipe, otherwise the panzanella will be soggy. To speed up the "staling" process, break the bread into chunks and put them in the oven to dry out.

The rolling green hills of the d'Orcia valley, around Pienza.

# MINESTRONE DI VERDURA CON FAGIOLI
### VEGETABLE AND BEAN SOUP

*Anna at the* Ristorante Roma *in Buonconvento cooks by judgement rather than by measuring out exact ingredients. Since* minestrone *means "jumble," feel free after a couple of tries to use a bit of culinary licence as far as quantities go.*

### SERVES 6

3 red onions, finely chopped
Extra-virgin olive oil
5 ripe tomatoes, peeled, or
1¼ cups *passata di pomodoro*
(crushed strained tomatoes)
3 carrots, finely chopped
2 celery stalks,
finely chopped
1 small white
cabbage, shredded
1 pound green cabbage
1 pound swiss chard
3 floury potatoes, peeled
and diced

Handful of fresh parsley,
finely chopped
3½ cups water
Salt and freshly ground
black pepper
3 firm zucchini,
thinly sliced
1½ cups dried *cannellini*
beans, soaked and cooked
4 ounces Parmesan cheese,
grated, to serve

1 In a large, heavy pan, fry the onions gently in olive oil until they have softened. Add the tomatoes and simmer for 10 minutes.

2 Stir in the carrots, celery, white and green cabbage, chard, potatoes, zucchini and parsley. Pour in the water and season well. Bring to a boil, then cover the pan and let the soup simmer gently over a low heat for 1½–2 hours.

3 Add the beans and check the seasoning, continue simmering for about 20 minutes more. Serve sprinkled with freshly grated Parmesan cheese.

# RIBOLLITA

## VEGETABLE SOUP WITH BREAD

*This peasant meal of twice-boiled vegetable soup (*ribollita *means "reboiled")
shows Tuscan food at its most frugal. Local farmworkers in San Gimignano used
to take their* ribollita *to the fields to reheat over a small fire for their midday meal.*

### SERVES 6

2 onions, finely chopped
Extra-virgin olive oil
3 carrots, finely chopped
3 large, floury
potatoes, chopped
4 celery stalks, chopped
1 pound green cabbage,
roughly chopped
3½ cups water
2 cups dried *cannellini*
beans, soaked and cooked

4 thick slices of stale, coarse
white bread, torn in chunks
Leaves of 1 fresh rosemary
sprig, finely chopped
Sea salt and freshly ground
black pepper
Finely chopped onion,
to garnish

1 In a large, heavy pan fry the onions gently in olive oil until they are golden.

2 Add the carrots, potatoes, celery and cabbage and cook for a few minutes, until the vegetables have softened. Cover with the water, bring to a boil, cover the pan, reduce the heat and simmer for an hour or so.

3 Purée half the beans and stir them into the soup, with the remaining beans, the bread, the rosemary and seasoning. Let the soup bubble for about 20 minutes or so, until the bread has been absorbed and the mixture has taken on the consistency of a thick broth.

4 Adjust the seasoning and serve very hot, with a little finely chopped raw onion and a drizzle of olive oil.

## Cook's Notes

*Like the minestrone in the preceding
recipe, ribollita is best made a day in advance,
to allow the flavours to develop.*

The indoor market in Florence typifies the abundance, freshness
and variety of Tuscan produce.

# ZUPPA DI CECI
## CHICK-PEA SOUP

*As this simple, nutritious soup uses only a few ingredients,*
*it relies for its success on really good olive oil and very fresh rosemary and garlic.*
*Make it for an informal winter supper, followed by a salad.*

### SERVES 4

4 garlic cloves
2 fresh rosemary sprigs
2½ cups dried chick-peas,
soaked overnight
3½ cups water
Cloudy extra-virgin olive oil

Coarse sea salt and freshly
ground black pepper
4 thick slices of coarse
white bread
3 ounces Parmesan cheese

1  Tie  the garlic cloves and rosemary sprigs in cheesecloth to make a bouquet garni. Cover the chick-peas and bouquet garni with the water. Boil vigorously, uncovered, for 10 minutes, then cover the pan, reduce the heat and simmer for about 1½ hours, or until the chick-peas are tender but not falling apart.

2  Remove the bouquet garni and mash the chick-peas until the soup has a thick, rough consistency.

3  Add ½ cup of good olive oil and plenty of seasoning.

4  Before serving, grill the bread and drizzle a little olive oil on each slice. Cut some Parmesan into shavings, using a vegetable peeler. Place one slice of the grilled bread on each bowl of soup and top with the Parmesan shavings.

# INSALATA DI FAGIOLI

## THREE BEAN SALAD

*Beans are so popular in Tuscany that Tuscans are known as*
mangiofagioli, *bean-eaters. This substantial salad makes a good lunch with*
*tomatoes, lettuce, crusty bread and a glass of red wine.*

### SERVES 6

2¼ cups cooked, drained
*borlotti* beans
2¼ cups cooked, drained
*cannellini* beans
2¼ cups cooked, drained
butter or lima beans
Cloudy extra-virgin olive oil
1 red onion, halved and
finely sliced
¼ cup pitted black olives,
halved

3–4 canned anchovy fillets,
finely chopped
4 tablespoons small capers,
rinsed and dried
Handful of fresh
parsley, chopped
Juice of 1 large lemon
1 teaspoon Dijon mustard
Sea salt and freshly ground
black pepper

1 Dress the beans in a generous amount of olive oil. Stir in the onion, olives, anchovies, capers and half the chopped parsley.

2 Dress with the lemon juice, mustard and plenty of seasoning. Cover and refrigerate for at least half an hour, to allow the dressing to be absorbed.

3 Toss the salad and adjust the seasoning to taste. Serve at room temperature, garnished with the remainder of the chopped parsley.

# TONNO E FAGIOLI

## CANNELLINI BEAN SALAD WITH RED ONION AND TUNA

*Tuna and beans form a substantial base to this popular salad and*
*the capers and red onion give it a bit of a kick. It's often eaten as an* antipasto,
*although a good helping makes a filling main course.*

### SERVES 4

4½ cups cooked, drained
*cannellini* beans
1 large can of tuna in olive
oil, drained and flaked
4 tablespoons small capers,
rinsed and dried
Cloudy extra-virgin olive oil

Italian red-wine vinegar or
lemon juice
Sea salt and freshly ground
black pepper
1 red onion, halved and
finely sliced

1 Mix together the beans, tuna and capers.

2 Dress with olive oil, vinegar or lemon juice and seasoning and top with the sliced red onion. Serve with crusty bread.

# Pisci al Ragù di Carne

## Homemade "pisci" with Meat Sauce

*This typically Tuscan pasta – a type of thick spaghetti – originated as a poor man's dish, since the proportion of egg to flour is much lower than usual for fresh pasta. Pisci-rolling is a little time consuming, so you may need to enlist a willing helper!*

### Serves 6

**For the Pasta**
3 cups all-purpose flour
Large pinch of salt
1 large egg
About ⅔ cup
tepid water

**For the Sauce**
Extra-virgin olive oil
1 onion, finely chopped
1 celery stalk, finely chopped
1 garlic clove, finely chopped
Small handful of fresh
parsley, chopped
2 carrots, finely chopped

12 ounces ground veal
12 ounces ground pork
Sea salt and freshly
ground black pepper
⅔ cup red wine
A 14-ounce can of plum
tomatoes, drained and finely
chopped
½ teaspoon sugar
3 tablespoons tomato paste
Grated Parmesan cheese,
to serve

1 Sift the flour into a bowl, with the salt, and mix in the lightly beaten egg. Add the tepid water gradually, until you have a soft, but not sticky, dough. Knead for a few minutes. Roll out very thinly on a floured surface. Allow to rest on the back of a chair for 30 minutes.

2 For the sauce, fry the onion, celery, garlic, parsley and carrots in a generous amount of olive oil for 10 minutes or until the onion is transparent. Transfer to a plate.

3 Heat some more olive oil over a higher heat and fry the meat until it is very brown. Return the vegetables to the pan and season (not too much salt as the tomato paste is salty). Reduce the heat and simmer the meat and vegetables for 20 minutes, adding more oil if necessary.

4 Pour in the wine and bubble until it evaporates. Add the tomatoes, sugar and tomato paste. Cover and simmer for 1–2 hours, checking that the sauce isn't drying out (if it is, add more tomatoes or wine – never add water).

5 Cut the pasta into ¼-inch strips. Using quick, light movements, roll each strip to form a spaghetti shape, about 12 inches in length and as thin as possible.

6 Put the pasta in lots of boiling salted water and cook for 4–5 minutes. Drain well, pour into a warmed dish and top with the sauce. Serve immediately, sprinkled with grated Parmesan cheese.

# Fagioli all'Ucceletto

### Cannellini Beans in Tomato, Garlic and Sage

*There are many suggestions as to why this dish is called "beans cooked like little birds." The most plausible is that* fagioli all'ucceletto *is the traditional accompaniment to* uccelletti – *little birds, which Tuscans love to eat.*

### Serves 4

4 cups dried *cannellini* beans, soaked overnight
A few tablespoons extra-virgin olive oil
Small sprig of fresh sage
3 garlic cloves, peeled and bruised

2 tablespoons tomato paste
Salt and pepper
2¼ cups vegetable stock

1 Cook the beans in slightly salted water for 40 minutes, or until they are tender. Drain.

2 Heat 3 tablespoons of oil and sauté the sage and bruised garlic for a couple of minutes, until the sage starts to brown. Discard the garlic. Stir in the tomato paste and some seasoning and then stir in the beans.

3 Cover with the vegetable stock and simmer for 10–15 minutes, stirring occasionally.

4 Transfer the beans to a dish and pour over a couple of tablespoons of good olive oil. Serve immediately.

# Rigatoni con Ricotta, Olive nere a Capperi

## Pasta with Ricotta Cheese, Black Olives and Capers

*This pasta dish is extremely quick to prepare. The succulent black olives and the capers counteract the blandness of the ricotta.*

### Serves 4

1 pound *rigatoni* dried pasta (large tubes)
A few tablespoons extra-virgin olive oil
½ cup ricotta cheese
¼ cup pitted black olives

7 tablespoons capers, rinsed, drained and chopped
Salt and freshly ground black pepper

1 Cook the pasta in lots of boiling salted water for 10 minutes, or until it is *al dente*. Drain.

2 Return the pasta to the pan and stir in 2 tablespoons of olive oil and then the ricotta and black olives. Season with salt and plenty of freshly ground black pepper.

3 Transfer to shallow bowls and scatter over the chopped capers.

*The medieval rooftops of San Gimignano*

# TAGLIATELLE AI CARCIOFI E PINOLI

## TAGLIATELLE WITH BABY ARTICHOKES AND PINE NUTS

*In spring and autumn, tightly packed purple artichokes on their long stems appear in the markets. Their tender inner leaves are dipped into unfiltered olive oil and eaten raw, or gently sautéed for thick omelets, or to eat with fresh tagliatelle.*

### SERVES 4

8 baby artichokes
A little lemon juice
3 ounces pine nuts
Extra-virgin olive oil
4 garlic cloves,
finely chopped
Small handful of fresh
parsley, finely chopped
Sea salt and freshly
ground black pepper

Few drops of truffle oil
1 pound fresh tagliatelle
(or dried)
Grated *pecorino stagionato*
(mature sheep's-milk
cheese), or Parmesan cheese,
to serve

1 To prepare the artichokes, remove the stalks and tough outer leaves, cut the artichokes into quarters and, with a small knife, remove any hairy choke in the center. Sprinkle with lemon juice to prevent discoloring.

2 Boil the artichokes in salted water for 6–7 minutes. Meanwhile, brown the pine nuts in a heavy frying pan.

3 Drain the artichokes and pat them dry. Sauté them in olive oil, with the garlic and parsley, for a few minutes, or until they are very tender.

4 Purée half the artichokes and stir in the pine nuts and seasoning. Stir in the remaining artichokes and drizzle over a few drops of truffle oil. Keep the sauce warm.

5 Cook the pasta in lots of boiling salted water for 6–7 minutes, or until it is *al dente*. Drain the pasta and mix it into the sauce. Serve immediately, sprinkled with the grated *pecorino* or Parmesan.

# Gnocchi al Pomodoro e Basilico

## POTATO GNOCCHI WITH TOMATO AND BASIL SAUCE

*Gnocchi are a classic winter dish, since they are both
deliciously warming and use up winter's old, floury potatoes. In Tuscany,
they are often eaten with a fragrant tomato and basil sauce.*

### SERVES 4

FOR THE GNOCCHI
1 pound unpeeled
floury potatoes
⅓ teaspoon salt
Yolks of 2 medium eggs
About 9 tablespoons flour,
sifted

FOR THE SAUCE
Extra-virgin olive oil
1 onion, finely chopped

2 garlic cloves,
finely chopped
1¼ cups *passata di pomodoro*
(crushed strained tomatoes)
Pinch of sugar
Sea salt and freshly ground
black pepper
1 cup fresh basil leaves
Grated Parmesan cheese,
to serve

1 For the sauce, fry the onion and garlic in olive oil for 10 minutes, until the onion is transparent. Stir in the *passata*, sugar, salt and pepper. Simmer, covered, for 30 minutes.

2 Cut the basil into shreds: the best way is to lay the leaves on top of each other, roll them to form a cigarette shape and slice them very finely, using a chef's knife. Stir them into the sauce.

3 For the *gnocchi*, boil the potatoes until they are tender. Drain them well and peel them (wear rubber gloves to avoid burning your fingers). While they are still hot, push them through a food mill or a wire strainer. Turn out onto a board. Working quickly, mix in the salt, egg yolks and enough of the flour to form a soft, elastic dough.

4 Divide the dough into workable portions. Roll each into a long sausage shape, the thickness of a finger. Cut each sausage into pieces just under 1 inch long (they will expand during cooking) and place them on a lightly floured tray.

5 Bring a pan of salted water to a boil. Drop the *gnocchi* in one by one and cook them for 3 minutes. Drain them carefully in a slotted spoon and transfer to a warmed, greased dish. Allow to rest in a warm oven for 2 minutes.

6 Add the sauce and mix carefully so as not to break the *gnocchi*. Sprinkle with Parmesan cheese and serve.

*Aprons drying in the brilliant morning sun.*

# TAGLIOLINI AI SETTE AROMI

## TAGLIOLINI WITH SEVEN FRESH HERBS

*Enrico Paradiso of the* Antica Trattoria *in Colle di Val d'Elsa is one of a group of respected restaurateurs who are re-introducing Renaissance flavors to Tuscan cooking. Here he combines seven wild herbs with* tagliolini, *a very thin spaghetti.*

### SERVES 4

4 ounces (about 2 cups) mixed fresh chives, mint, tarragon, chervil, basil, marjoram and parsley
Sea salt and freshly ground black pepper
¼ cup extra-virgin olive oil

4 ripe plum tomatoes, peeled and finely chopped, or a can of plum tomatoes, drained, chopped and drained again
1 pound fresh or dried *tagliolini* (preferably fresh)

1 Chop all the herbs finely and mash them in a mortar and pestle with some salt and freshly ground black pepper. Stir in the olive oil. Cook gently for 5 minutes.

2 Add the chopped tomatoes, cover and simmer for 10 minutes more. Check the seasoning.

3 Cook the *tagliolini* in lots of boiling salted water until *al dente*, 2–3 minutes – do not overcook them or they will be ruined. Drain them quickly and toss them into the sauce. Serve immediately, topped with more freshly ground black pepper.

*Golden harvested wheatfields, Colle di Val d'Elsa, with the promise of fresh bread to come.*

# Ravioli con Spinaci e Ricotta

### Fresh Ravioli with Spinach and Ricotta Stuffing

*Fresh pasta is made every morning at the* Trattoria La Torre *in Siena and carefully laid out on a checked tablecloth, between the pasta-boiling pot and the guests' tables. Wild sage from the surrounding hills gives a perfumed finish to the dish.*

### Serves 4

**FOR THE PASTA**
1¼ cups all-purpose flour
2 large eggs
A little warm water

**FOR THE FILLING**
8 ounces spinach,
cooked, well drained and
finely chopped
1 cup ricotta cheese
2 tablespoons extra-virgin
olive oil

Large pinch of freshly
grated nutmeg
Sea salt and freshly ground
black pepper

**TO DRESS THE RAVIOLI**
4 tablespoons butter
Few fresh sage leaves
3 ounces Parmesan
cheese, grated

1 Sift the flour onto a clean surface and make a high-walled well in the middle. Crack the eggs into the well and start to beat them in with your fingers, gradually incorporating the flour from the inside of the well. Add warm water, a spoonful at a time, until you have a soft, but not sticky, dough.

2 Knead gently for a few minutes. Cover loosely and leave to rest in a cool place for half an hour.

3 Meanwhile, mix together all the ingredients for the ravioli filling.

4 Roll out the dough lightly and quickly to a thickness of about ⅛ inch. Cut into rectangles approximately 2 × 4 inches.

5 Place a heaping teaspoonful of filling on half of each piece of dough and fold over the other half to make a sandwich. Seal the edges of the ravioli with wet fingers.

6 Cook for 4–5 minutes in lots of boiling salted water.

7 Melt the butter with the sage leaves. As soon as the ravioli are cooked, remove them from the water with a perforated metal spoon, dress with the butter and sage and serve immediately, sprinkled with freshly grated Parmesan and black pepper.

Florence's celebrated *bistecca alla Fiorentina* – grilled T-bone steak – is Tuscan cooking at its best: simple, graceful, yet requiring art and skill to make it just so. To the Tuscan chef, making a perfect *bistecca* is like a French chef making a perfect omelet – the task is taken seriously. Everybody has their own ideas about the technicalities: timing, how the smoke wafts, the distance between the meat and the embers, when and how much oil to drizzle over.

A true *Fiorentina* steak should come from the Chianina

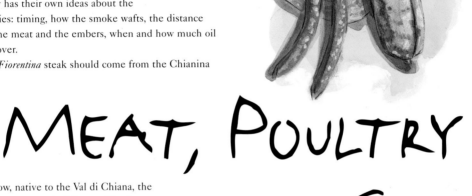

# Meat, Poultry and Game

breed of cow, native to the Val di Chiana, the lush valley to the south of Arezzo. Tender and well marbled with fat, it retains its succulence when grilled and takes the aromatic flavors of embers, often scented with pine or juniper. Only once it is cooked is the steak drizzled with the tiniest drop of the finest green olive oil. Val di Chiana beef is only available in Italy, but one Tuscan chef I spoke to conceded that Aberdeen Angus beef could be used instead.

The tender, plump, corn-fed chickens reared in Tuscany are also shown off at their best when grilled. Small chickens are halved, then cooked *alla diavola*: over charcoal, with sage, rosemary and garlic. The rich, dense chicken livers are used for a coarse pâté flavored with capers, to spread thickly on *crostini* as appetizers.

For large pieces of succulent meat, the spit-roast *porchetta*, or young suckling pig, is the prime candidate. Tuscans still believe that *Se non c'e porchetta, non c'e festa*

"there's no celebration if there's not a porchetta." To make *porchetta*, a whole pig, weighing as much as 130 pounds is boned, stuffed with a mixture of minced herbs, garlic and salt and slowly roasted. It is still popular at Tuscan markets, thick slices stuffed into crusty rolls and eaten as people stroll around. Loin of pork is also boned and stuffed with rosemary and garlic and spit-roasted, or roasted in the oven with wine (*arista di maiale*). Lamb does not feature widely in Tuscany, the animals being valued for their milk to make *pecorino* cheese. At Easter time, however, tender young spring lamb, studded with rosemary and garlic, is cooked on the spit-roast.

MIXED-MEAT STEWS

For cheaper cuts of meat, slow stewing *in umido* – in vegetables and wine – is favored. Some of the meat stews of the *cucina povera* tradition date back to more frugal times, when the country folk would make use of what was available. Around the region evolved *scottiglia* – a mixed-meat stew cooked for a neighboring get-together, when each would bring what they had: chicken, rabbit, pork, pigeon and guinea fowl. Everything was thrown into the stewing pot, with vegetables and wine. *Stracotto*, which literally means "overcooked," and *peposo* are tender beef stews using cheap but tasty cuts of meat.

The woods of Tuscany abound with game: pheasant, partridge, rabbit, hare and wild boar, are all important parts of the Tuscan diet. To bring out flavor and tenderize, game, too, is usually stewed slowly. Its distinctive flavors are complemented by Renaissance-inspired *agrodolce* sauces, combining sweet and savory flavors.

Pheasant is stewed in sweet

*vin santo* wine, with grapes; guinea fowl cooked with prunes and pine nuts; hare with cloves. Wild boar is even cooked with chocolate – in the tiniest quantity – to give sweetness, color and substance to the sauce.

Arezzo's famous dish is *pappardelle alla lepre*, hare sauce served with flat, wide noodles. It has been eaten since medieval times, when peasants, forbidden to hunt or shoot, would use the blood and other parts of the hare not required for the master's table to make a rich sauce.

Tripe, the ultimate poor-man's food, is still popular. At a stall behind the Piazza della Signoria in Florence, people line up daily for freshly boiled tripe *alla Fiorentina*, with a dressing of garlic and capers, drizzled with olive oil and salt and stuffed into crusty bread.

There are numerous pork and boar products in Tuscany. Pure pork sausages – the fatty *capocollo* made from the pig's head, or the leaner *luganega* or *cotechino* – are stewed with beans as *salsicce e fagioli*, or with lentils (*con lenticchie*), in a special dish eaten on New Year's Eve to invoke prosperity for the coming year. These sausages can be found in Italian stores. In Arezzo, butchers make their sausages with ginger, *allo zenzero*.

The favorite *salame* is *finocchiona*, a fairly fatty, loosely packed *salame* with wild fennel or fennel seeds. Every town store sells locally produced *prosciutto* – lean, salty and delicious when eaten together with mild sheep's-milk cheese and unsalted bread. *Prosciutto sotto cenere* – ham which has been preserved by the ancient method of burying it under wood embers – is still sold in some places. The wild boar that inhabit the Maremma are hunted between October and December. So that Tuscans can enjoy boar – *cinghiale* – for the rest of the year, hams, salami and sausages, are made. These can be found in every town's food shop.

Cool, dark osterie in the narrow streets around the Ponte Vecchio are said to serve the juiciest steaks in Florence.

# Prosciutto Crudo con Fichi

## Prosciutto with Purple Figs

*In late summer, wild purple figs are served as an antipasto*
*or light lunch with thin slices of locally cured ham. The figs' sweet, seeded*
*insides are a perfect balance to the saltiness of the soft ham.*

### Serves 4

4 large, ripe, purple figs
6 ounces *prosciutto crudo*, thinly sliced

1 With a small knife, make four incisions from the top to the base of each fig, without cutting it right through. Carefully peel back the sections to form petals.

2 Arrange the figs on a plate around the slices of ham.

*This formidable boar's head is the guardian of the prosciutto shop, Siena.*

# CROSTINI DI FEGATELLI DI POLLO
## CHICKEN LIVER CROSTINI

*Pieces of country bread, grilled, drizzled with a little oil and then topped with many types of delicacy, are served throughout Tuscany as appetizers. The most popular* crostini, *Florentine in origin, are made with chicken livers and capers.*

**SERVES 4**

1 medium onion, finely chopped
2 garlic cloves, finely chopped
Extra-virgin olive oil
8 ounces chicken livers
¼ cup dry Marsala or port

Coarse sea salt and freshly ground black pepper
20 thin slices of baguette
Handful of tiny capers, rinsed and drained, to garnish

1 Gently fry the onion and garlic in olive oil for a few minutes, until the onion has softened. Remove them from the pan with a slotted spoon and reserve them.

2 In more olive oil, quickly fry the chicken livers over a high heat until they are brown on all sides. Season generously. Add the Marsala or port and leave everything to bubble for a few minutes, until nearly all the liquid has evaporated. Stir in the fried onions and garlic. Check the seasoning.

3 Blend in a food processor for a few seconds, until the pâté is spreadable but still rough in texture. Let cool.

4 Brown the baguette slices on both sides. Drizzle a drop of olive oil on each slice.

5 Spread the *crostini* immediately before serving, and garnish with the capers.

# POLLO ALLA DIAVOLA

## GRILLED MARINATED CHICKEN

*Tuscan chickens, fed on corn, are considered the best in Italy. This dish is usually prepared on an open fire over hot embers, but a cast-iron griddle will also do the job. Serve with sautéed spinach (see page 69) and grilled polenta (page 71).*

**SERVES 4**

| | |
|---|---|
| 2 small chickens (preferably corn-fed), weighing about 2¼ pounds each | Leaves of 2–3 rosemary sprigs |
| Juice of 2 lemons | Small handful of sage leaves |
| 4 cloves of garlic, peeled and sliced | Extra-virgin olive oil |
| | Sea salt and freshly ground black pepper |

1 Cut both chickens down the middle to make four pieces in all. Pound the pieces with a rolling pin so that they lie flat.

2 Mix the lemon juice, garlic, rosemary, sage, salt and pepper, olive oil. Cover the chicken pieces with this marinade and leave for an hour.

3 Preheat a griddle for 5 minutes until it is extremely hot. Put the chicken pieces on the griddle and leave for 2 minutes, until the skin is charred with the markings of the griddle. Brown the chicken on the other side.

4 Reduce the heat a little and pour over the marinade, a little at a time, keeping the herbs on top of the chicken to prevent their burning.

5 To allow the meat to cook through evenly and retain its moisture, press it down with a heavy iron pan. Continue to cook, turning occasionally, for 25–30 minutes until the juices in the thigh run clear when pressed.

# PETTI DI POLLO AL TARTUFO E FUNGHI PORCINI

CHICKEN BREASTS WITH TRUFFLES AND PORCINI MUSHROOMS

*Late autumn is when fresh truffles are hunted, using pigs, from
the oak woods around Monte Amiata. Truffles have a powerful, sensual aroma
that marries well with the rich earthiness of wild mushrooms.*

SERVES 4

4 boneless, skinless chicken
breasts (preferably corn-fed)
6 tablespoons butter
4 ounces fresh *porcini*
mushrooms, or ¼ ounce dried
*porcini*, soaked for 2 hours in
warm water
⅔ cup milk

1½ ounces fresh, canned or
preserved white truffles,
grated, or 3 teaspoons
truffle purée
Few drops of truffle oil
Sea salt and freshly ground
black pepper

1 Sauté the chicken breasts in half the butter until they are pale golden on both sides. Add the *porcini* mushrooms and brown them in a little more of the butter.

2 In a separate pan, heat the remaining butter with the milk, grated truffles or truffle purée and truffle oil.

3 Pour the sauce over the chicken and *porcini*, season and cook very gently for 4–5 minutes, turning the chicken halfway through.

4 Transfer the chicken to a warmed plate and reduce the sauce for a couple of minutes until it thickens.

## Cook's Notes

Fresh truffles are available only between November and February and are prohibitively expensive even before being exported; a good alternative for this dish would be canned or preserved truffles or truffle purée.

*Chickens scratching in the sunshine on a farm in Greve in Chianti.*

# FARAONA ALLA MEDICI

## GUINEA FOWL "MEDICI-STYLE"

*Sumptuous dishes combining meat with dried fruit, nuts and herbs*
*were popular served at banquets in the medieval period, and this festive dish*
*was apparently a favorite of Catherine de' Medici's.*

This fourteenth-century fresco from Siena shows the unchanging
tranquillity of the Tuscan countryside.

### SERVES 4

Extra-virgin olive oil
2 small guinea fowl
Rosemary sprig
Few sage leaves
2 small onions,
finely chopped
2 carrots, finely chopped
1 celery stalk, finely chopped
Flour
Half a bottle of
*Chianti Classico*
6 ounces prunes,
pitted
½ cup pine nuts
¾ cup whole almonds
Sea salt and freshly ground
black pepper

1 Preheat the oven to 400°F. Heat oil in a frying pan and brown the meat with the rosemary and sage. Transfer everything to a deep casserole and roast the meat for 30 minutes.

2 Meanwhile, gently fry the onions, carrots and celery in more olive oil.

3 After the 30 minutes roasting time, remove and coat the meat lightly with flour and put it back in the casserole with the softened vegetables, wine, prunes, pine nuts, almonds and seasoning. Cover the casserole with a tightly fitting lid and return to the oven for 35–40 minutes, basting every 10 minutes or so, until the meat is tender and the sauce has thickened. Serve with cooked *cannellini* beans dressed with olive oil (see page 45).

# Coniglio Alla Cacciatora

## HUNTER-STYLE RABBIT

*There are many varieties of sauce to serve with rabbit and game. This one is from*
*Alberto's* Ristorante il Giardino *in Montalcino. He serves the rabbit with oaky*
Rosso di Montalcino, *the younger version of the famous* Brunello di Montalcino.

### SERVES 4–5

1 rabbit, cut into 8 pieces
(ask your butcher to do this)
Extra-virgin olive oil
1 large onion, finely chopped
1 carrot, finely chopped
2 celery stalks,
finely chopped
Bunch of fresh parsley,
finely chopped

2 ripe tomatoes, peeled and
roughly chopped
1 small green chile pepper,
seeded and
finely chopped
Bottle of Tuscan
*vino da tavola*
Sea salt and freshly ground
black pepper

### Cook's Notes

As with many meat dishes cooked in wine,
these flavours will continue to develop for a day or two,
so make this dish in advance if you can.

1 Wash the rabbit pieces and pat them dry. Brown them in olive oil and then remove to a plate.

2 Fry the onion, carrot, celery and parsley in a generous amount of olive oil for a few minutes until they have softened. Add the browned meat, chopped tomatoes, wine, chopped chile and seasoning.

3 Bring to a boil, reduce the heat and simmer, covered, for an hour, or until the meat is tender. Cook, uncovered, for 15 minutes more, to reduce the sauce.
Serve with *cannellini* beans, dressed with good olive oil.

# Coniglio al Brunello

## RABBIT IN BRUNELLO WITH PANCETTA AND WILD SAGE

*On the road to Monte Amiata lies the* Fattoria dei Barbi, *a working farm famed for its excellent restaurant and its* Brunello di Montalcino *wine. This colorful, aromatic stew is served here with a delicate pale green dish of sautéed fennel (see page 66).*

**SERVES 4**

1 rabbit, cut into 8 pieces
(ask your butcher to do this)
2 red onions
8 ounces smoked *pancetta*
(smoked belly of pork)
Large handful of fresh
sage leaves

Extra-virgin olive oil
1 bottle *Brunello di
Montalcino*, or *Rosso di
Montalcino*, or *Chianti Classico*
½ teaspoon sugar
Sea salt and freshly ground
black pepper

1 Wash the rabbit pieces and pat them dry.

2 In a blender, chop the onion, *pancetta* and sage finely. Sauté in a generous amount of olive oil for 10 minutes, stirring occasionally. Add the rabbit pieces and brown them on both sides.

3 Cover the meat with the wine and season with sugar, salt and pepper. Bring to a boil, cover the pan with a tightly fitting lid and reduce the heat.

4 Simmer for an hour, stirring every 10 minutes or so, until the meat is very tender.

# Ossobuco alla Sienese

## Braised Shanks of Veal

*This Sienese version of the classic* ossobuco Milanese *uses garlic and chile pepper to give the dish a little punch.* Ossobucco *literally means "hole in the bone" – the creamy marrow inside the bone is thought to be a particular delicacy.*

### Serves 4

4 garlic cloves, finely chopped
1 medium red chile pepper, seeded and very finely chopped
Extra-virgin olive oil
4 veal shanks, weighing 8 ounces each
Flour

¾ cup white wine
1 pound ripe plum tomatoes, peeled, de-seeded and chopped, or canned plum tomatoes, drained and chopped
Pinch of sugar
1⅓ cups beef stock

1 Fry the chopped garlic and chile pepper gently in olive oil until the garlic has colored a little. Remove to a plate.

2 Dust the veal shanks with flour. Brown them on both sides in olive oil. Return the garlic and chile to the pan.

3 Add the wine and simmer for 10 minutes. Add the chopped tomatoes and pinch of sugar, then pour in the beef stock to cover the meat.

4 Bring to a boil, cover the pan and cook very gently for an hour, or until the veal shanks are so tender that the meat is almost falling off the bone. Serve with potato purée or crusty bread to mop up the sauce, and any vegetable dish.

Drummers at the Palio, the annual horse-race that recreates medieval Siena.

## Cook's Notes

Ossobuco is a cut of meat which responds particularly well to slow stewing: at the end of cooking time, it should be so tender that it can be cut with a spoon. During the cooking, make sure the meat is always covered with liquid (add more wine or tomatoes if necessary) and allow enough cooking time.

# LENTICCHIE CON SALSICCE

## SAUSAGES WITH BROWN LENTILS

*This rustic winter dish mixes pure pork sausages with the tiny brown lentils that grow on the highland plans of neighboring Umbria. Lentils are eaten with sausages on New Year's Eve in Tuscany and many other regions of Italy.*

### SERVES 4

1½ pounds pure
pork sausages
2½ cups small brown lentils,
well rinsed
2 celery stalks,
finely chopped

2 garlic cloves,
finely chopped
6 tablespoons extra-virgin
olive oil
Sea salt and freshly ground
black pepper

1 Brown the sausages under a hot broiler.

2 Put the lentils in a deep, heavy casserole with the browned sausages, chopped celery, garlic, olive oil and seasoning. Cover with water.

3 Bring to a boil, reduce the heat and simmer slowly for an hour, or until the lentils are tender but not falling apart. Serve very hot.

The mysterious beauty of winter in the Casella valley.

# FILETTI DI MAIALE AL GINEPRO CON PURÉE DI PATATE

## PORK TENDERLOIN IN JUNIPER BERRIES WITH PURÉED POTATOES

*Aromatic berries and oaky wine make an autumnal meal out*
*of good pork tenderloin. Creamy potatoes take advantage of the rich sauce,*
*produced by the slow simmering of the marinade juices.*

### SERVES 4

4 thin slices of pork
tenderloin, weighing about
4 ounces each
Half a bottle of
*Chianti Classico*
2 fresh rosemary sprigs
3 teaspoons juniper berries,
very lightly crushed
3 teaspoons sugar
4 tablespoons butter
Sea salt and freshly ground
black pepper

FOR THE PURÉED POTATOES
2 pounds floury potatoes,
peeled and quartered
4 tablespoons butter
⅔ cup milk
Freshly grated nutmeg
Sea salt and freshly ground
black pepper

1 Three hours in advance, marinate the meat in the wine, rosemary, juniper berries, sugar and salt and pepper.

2 Strain the marinade into a bowl, discarding the sprigs of rosemary, and pat the meat dry.

3 Heat the butter in a heavy frying pan and brown the pork slices on both sides. Add the marinade. Bring to a boil, then cover, reduce the heat and simmer gently for 20 minutes. Check the seasoning.

4 For the purée, boil the potatoes until they are very tender. Drain well and then beat in the butter, milk, nutmeg and lots of seasoning.

# CINGHIALE IN AGRODOLCE

### WILD BOAR IN SWEET AND SOUR SAUCE

*The wild boar of the Maremma are hunted each winter for sport
and for the table. Traditional game dishes often include the unlikely ingredient of
chocolate, which sweetens, colors and thickens the sauce.*

### SERVES 4

1 pound boneless leg of wild
boar, cut into fairly
large pieces
Half a bottle of oaky red
wine
2 garlic cloves, sliced
1 onion, finely sliced
2–3 rosemary sprigs
Extra-virgin olive oil

Sea salt and freshly ground
black pepper
½ cup pine nuts
2 tablespoons sugar
2 tablespoons white-wine
vinegar
1 ounce bittersweet
chocolate, grated
½ cup raisins

1 One day in advance, cover the boar pieces with a marinade of the wine, garlic, onion and rosemary.

2 On the serving day, drain the marinade into a bowl, discarding the rosemary, and pat the meat dry.

3 Brown the meat in olive oil in a heavy casserole. Add the onions and garlic from the marinade liquid. Stir for a couple of minutes and then add the liquid and seasoning. Bring to a boil, cover the casserole, reduce the heat and simmer for one hour, stirring occasionally, until the meat is tender.

4 Toast the pine nuts in the oven, or in a dry frying pan, until golden. Heat the sugar in a heavy pan with a tablespoon of water until caramelized, making sure it does not burn, then immediately add the vinegar. Mix to a syrupy consistency and add the grated chocolate. Stir this sauce into the meat, with the raisins and pine nuts. Cook gently for 15 minutes more. Grilled polenta (page 71) is a good accompaniment, because its blandness offsets the richness of the dish.

# AGNELLO ARROSTO

### ROAST LEG OF SPRING LAMB WITH ROSEMARY AND GARLIC

*Spring lamb is an Easter dish in Tuscany, a tradition probably dating back to Judaeo-Christian custom. The spit-roast, which gives a crisp, salted outside, is ideal for young, tender meat; roasting at high temperature will achieve a very similar effect.*

### SERVES 3–4

| | |
|---|---|
| 1 small leg of spring lamb | Sea salt and freshly ground |
| Leaves of 3 fresh rosemary | black pepper |
| sprigs, finely chopped | Olive oil |
| 4 fat garlic cloves, chopped | ⅓ cup red wine |

1 Preheat the oven to its highest setting. Pat the meat dry.

2 Pound the rosemary and garlic together in a mortar and pestle, with salt, black pepper and a little olive oil. Make some incisions on either side of the leg and stuff them with this mixture.

3 Rub the outside of the meat with olive oil and place it on a rack set over a roasting tin. This will allow air to circulate around the meat during the cooking.

4 Place at the top of the oven for about 15 minutes, to seal the meat, turning it halfway through, and cook until both sides of the leg are brown.

5 Reduce the heat to 375°F. Allow a further 15 minutes per pound for slightly pink lamb or 20 minutes per pound for more well cooked lamb. During this time, baste every 10 minutes with a little olive oil and some coarse sea salt. Fifteen minutes before the end, remove the rack and place the meat onto the roasting pan, where juices will have collected. Pour over the wine and finish the cooking.

6 Baste the lamb with the collected juices, and leave it in a warm place to rest for 10 minutes before carving. To preserve its tenderness, young lamb is cut off the bone in chunks rather than carved. The usual accompaniment is the new season's fresh fava beans, *fave*, sautéed in good olive oil with garlic and wild sage.

*Hillside sheep, Monte Amiata, forage for the herbs that give their cheese its sweetness.*

## Cook's Notes

Outside the new lamb season, older leg of lamb – which is less tender but excellent in flavour – can be roasted by this method; you will need to brown the leg in oil first, cover it with pancetta (belly of pork) and baste it frequently, to prevent it from drying out.

The Ligurian Sea along Tuscany's coastline is home to a wealth of fish and seafood. Everywhere – from the beaches of Viareggio in the North to the fishing village of Ortobello in the South – fish is prepared simply, allowing its true flavor to come through. Favorite methods are grilling over chestnut wood, frying and stewing in tomato sauce: *in zimino*. Sauces, other than the simplest – made only of fresh tomatoes, wine and wild herbs – are deemed unnecessary.

The famous fish soup of Livorno – *cacciucco* – contains just about every fish that swims in these waters. Originally a fisherman's dish, this gargantuan soup came about to use up bits and pieces from the morning's catch. They say that to make a good *cacciucco* you need at least as many types of fish as there are Cs in the name. Different pieces of fish in varying sizes and textures are dropped into a basic sauce of onion, carrot, celery, wine and tomatoes – the most delicate fish last. There will be *orata* (sea bream), *scorfani* (scorpion fish), huge sea eels (*morene*), dentex (*dentice*) and other local fish, some with obscure names like *batti batti*. In a less famous Livorno soup – *bavettine sul pesce* – a paste of mashed mixed fish is stirred into a fish broth and, finally, fine noodles (*bavettine*) are added as it is

# FISH AND SEAFOOD

brought to a brief boil. These are both difficult dishes to reproduce outside the region, since these meaty rock fish are so local, so the recipes are not included here. Livorno's other speciality is red mullet (*triglie*) the scaly fish found in the deep rocky waters off the

shores. These are fried in olive oil or grilled whole – the liver left in as an extra delicacy – and topped with a rich tomato sauce.

Tuscans generally regard sea bass (*spigola*) as the most beautiful and delicate fish of the sea, and treat it accordingly. It is usually marinated briefly in white-wine vinegar, then simmered with garlic, onion and bay leaves. Alternatively, the fish is cut into pieces and braised *in agrodolce*, in a sweet-sour sauce with bacon.

Down in Piombino, *polpo alla Piombinese* – chopped reef octopus cooked in its own juices and plenty of chiles – is eaten from stalls as a street snack. Tender baby octopus (*moscardini*) are stewed slowly *in zimino*, in tomato sauce. The classic *risotto nero* – rice made black with squid ink and studded with pieces of squid and chopped spinach beet – is made all along the coast.

In Tuscany, not only baby eels are appreciated(see box below). The mature animal is also fished from the Arno and its tributaries, and enjoyed in a variety of imaginative ways. Chief among them are *agnello alla Fiorentina*, in which the eel is cut into pieces, fried in sage-flavored oil, baked in white or red wine, then finished off with breadcrumbs under a broiler, or *all'arentina*, made into kabobs interspersed with bread cubes and thyme, and basted with olive oil while being grilled. A cold speciality, *agnello marinate*, is sometimes encountered. In this dish, the eel pieces are first floured and fried, then left to mascerate in spiced vinegar. Across the waters in Tuscany's mountainous island of Elba, sardines (*sardine*) and anchovies (*acciughe*) are marinated in wine, garlic and chillies and then grilled over pine embers on an outdoor fire; sea salmon and swordfish are more upmarket choices. Squid is popular too, either

stuffed or stewed in its own ink as an *antipasto*. Elban folklore has it that Napoleon, during his exile here, loved to eat *seppie con carciofi*, squid with artichokes.

All along the coastline, the fishmarkets display jet-black, tightly closed mussels and cream-colored clams. Though the universal Italian term for mussels is *cozze*, local Tuscan names include *telline* (also, confusingly, used sometimes for clams) and *muscoli*. Whatever they are called, they will be steamed and then thrown together with garlic, tomatoes and chopped parsley for *spaghetti alla marinara*. Mussels are also stuffed with parsley, breadcrumbs and Parmesan cheese – *cozze ripiene* – and served as appetizers.

In Arezzo, glistening trout fished from the Arno, are cooked *affogate* or "drowned": first sautéed in butter and then cooked through in white wine.

Inland, fish has not played a huge role in cooking. In the past, restricted transport between regions meant that fresh fish was difficult, if not impossible, to come by, and so, for Fridays and obligatory Lenten dishes, preserved cod would be used. Either salted as *baccalà* or dried in the sun and

## SMALL IS BEAUTIFULLY DELICIOUS

Along Tuscany's gently undulating coast, eels feature on restaurant menus and in home cooking. In late winter and early spring, the incoming tide of the Arno boils with tiny elvers (*cieche*) – transparent baby eels – which are regarded as a particular delicacy around Pisa. Old culinary tomes describe the night-fishing expeditions which took place on warm late February and March nights. Bobbing and winking lanterns recorded the progress of the elvermen along the banks, as they skimmed the water with long-handled sieves. Nowadays, as everywhere else, such natural bounty is becoming scarcer and, as a result, increasingly

expensive. While better-off cooks and top restaurants splurge on the seasonal extravagance, thrifty housewives substitute transparent goby – *rossetto* – a far more common little fish. Whether cooking cieche or rossetto, the fish are first fried in olive oil, then either baked under a crust of Parmesan, breadcrumbs, egg and lemon juice until golden, or gently stewed in tomato sauce topped with Parmesan.

The northern coastal town of Livorno prefers new-born sardines and anchovies (*bianchetti* – "little white ones") whose jelly-like consistency turns creamy when stirred gently in a frying pan with eggs and lemon.

The bronzed fishermen of Grossetto return with their succulent catch which will be turned into delicacies for the Tuscan table.

wind as *stoccafisso*, it required lengthy and patient preparation. Nowadays, fresh fish is available in most parts of inland Tuscany but *baccalà* and *stoccafisso* are still very popular, cooked in tomato sauce with olives, stewed slowly with raisins and pine nuts, or lightly coated in flour and fried.

Bottled or canned tuna is also much in evidence, though in its best incarnations it bears little resemblance to that made familiar by our supermarkets. Beautiful strips of white albacore tuna are preserved in olive oil, and decanted to add to a variety of salads, including the ubiquitous *fagioli con tonno* (cannellini beans with tuna), as well as to sliced cold potatoes, and to hard-boiled eggs and capers. *Polpettone di tonno* (tuna loaf flavored with Parmesan) is also an easily prepared antipasto; its cold slices, decorated with mayonnaise and tomato, are found gracing many an *al fresco* summer lunch.

# Acciughe Ripieni

STUFFED FRESH ANCHOVIES

*The delicate flavor of these tiny fish from the Ligurian coast is
enhanced by a fragrant green stuffing. A dish of freshly cooked bite-sized anchovies
makes a perfect summer appetizer, served with chilled dry white wine.*

### SERVES 4

8 ounces fresh anchovies,
boned, cleaned and dried
1 ounce Parmesan cheese,
grated
1 garlic clove
Handful of parsley
⅔ cup fresh white bread
crumbs

Sea salt and freshly ground
black pepper
Extra-virgin olive oil
Flour, seasoned
1 egg, beaten
Lemon wedges, to serve

1 For the stuffing, blend a quarter of the anchovies with the Parmesan, garlic and parsley and stir in the bread crumbs, seasoning and add a little olive oil to moisten the mixture.

2 Stuff the remaining anchovies with this mixture. Dip them into the seasoned flour and then into the egg.

3 Fry the anchovies in a little olive oil for one minute on each side, or until they are brown.

4 Serve immediately, sprinkled with a little lemon juice.

*Terraced hillsides by the Ligurian sea ensure that every inch of land contributes its yield.*

# Linguine con Seppie

## LINGUINE WITH SQUID AND WINE SAUCE

*Squid is deliciously tender when it is stewed in a good sauce,
as in this recipe. Fresh squid is excellent and good fishmongers will be
happy to clean them – a fiddly business – for you.*

### SERVES 4

1½ pounds squid, cleaned
4 garlic cloves,
finely chopped
1 small fresh red chile
pepper,
seeded and finely chopped
Extra-virgin olive oil
1¼ cups dry white wine
3¼ pounds ripe plum
tomatoes, peeled, seeded and
chopped,

or 2 cans of plum tomatoes,
drained and chopped, mixed
with 1 teaspoon sugar
Large handful of fresh
parsley, chopped
Sea salt and freshly ground
black pepper
1 pound dried *linguine*
(flat spaghetti)

1 Slice the squid into thin rings and then wash them thoroughly and pat dry.

2 Gently fry the chopped garlic and chile in olive oil for a couple of minutes. Add the squid and cook for 10 minutes, stirring.

3 Add the wine and let the mixture bubble for a couple of minutes. Stir in the tomatoes and parsley. Bring to the boil, cover the pan, reduce the heat and simmer for an hour, or until the squid is very tender and the sauce has reduced. Season to taste.

4 Cook the *linguine* in lots of boiling salted water for about 8 minutes; they should be only just *al dente*. Drain the *linguine* and stir into the sauce for the final 2–3 minutes of cooking time. Serve immediately.

# Triglie Grigliate

GRILLED RED MULLET WITH PARSLEY AND GARLIC STUFFING

*These firm-fleshed fish are found in the deep, rocky waters of the Ligurian Sea, off the coast of Tuscany. When very fresh, their color is so vibrant that it seems a shame to do anything other than grill them simply with garlic and herbs.*

SERVES 4

| | |
|---|---|
| 4 whole red mullet, weighing approximately 8 ounces each, gutted and cleaned | Small handful of fresh parsley, very finely chopped |
| 3 garlic cloves, very finely chopped | Extra-virgin olive oil |
| | Sea salt and freshly ground black pepper |

1 Dry the fish well with paper towels. Pound the chopped garlic and parsley with a little olive oil, salt and pepper. Make three incisions on each side of the fish and stuff them with the garlic and parsley mixture.

2 Brush both sides of each fish with a little more olive oil. Grill for 3–4 minutes on each side, until the fish is golden on the outside and white in the middle. Serve with sautéd spinach (see page 69), for a stunning color contrast.

# Sogliola al Limone

FRIED SOLE WITH LEMON

*This wonderfully simple recipe is from the small* Ristorante La Torre, *behind the Piazza del Campo in Siena. The sole are fried very quickly one at a time and served with a tomato and lettuce salad.*

SERVES 4

| | |
|---|---|
| Olive oil | Sea salt and freshly ground black pepper |
| 4 very fresh whole medium sole, gutted and cleaned | 1 lemon, cut in wedges, to serve |
| Flour, seasoned | |
| ⅔ cup dry white wine | |

1 Dry the fish well with paper towels. Coat each fish with seasoned flour, shaking off the excess.

2 Heat a thin layer of good olive oil over a very high heat. When it is bubbling, add the fish and shallow-fry for a couple of minutes on each side until it is browned.

3 Add half the wine and cook until evaporated. Turn the fish and do the same again with the remaining wine. The fish should be crisp outside and very tender inside.

4 Serve immediately, garnished with the lemon wedges.

# Spaghetti alla Marinara

## Spaghetti with Mussels and Clams

*Mussels and clams are found all along the Tuscan coast and this is a popular summer dish in the Maremma and Elba. Steaming the mussels and clams in their own liquid allows them to retain a good deal of the flavor of the sea.*

### Serves 4

2 garlic cloves,
finely chopped
1 small red chile pepper,
seeded and finely chopped
Extra-virgin olive oil
1⅓ cups dry white wine
12 ounces ripe tomatoes,
peeled and chopped, or
canned plum tomatoes,
drained and chopped

Handful of fresh parsley,
finely chopped
Sea salt and freshly ground
black pepper
1 pound spaghetti
8 ounces live mussels,
scrubbed and de-bearded
8 ounces live
clams, scrubbed

1 Gently fry the garlic and chile in a generous amount of olive oil until everything is soft.

2 Pour in the wine and cook for a few minutes, until half the liquid has evaporated. Then add the tomatoes, chopped parsley and seasoning. Cover the pan, and simmer for 20 minutes.

3 Bring a large pan of salted water to a boil, and put in the pasta to cook. (It will take about 8 minutes.)

4 Discard any mussels or clams that don't close when tapped sharply. Put the mussels and clams into a large pan over a fairly high heat and cover to allow them to steam in their own liquid. Take the lid off as soon as they start to open (a couple of minutes) and continue to steam for 2–3 minutes. Discard any mussels or clams that don't open. Tip the mussels, clams and their liquid into the tomato sauce and let simmer.

5 Drain the pasta when it is still 2–3 minutes off being *al dente* and stir it into the sauce.

# TROTA ALLA SALVIA

### PAN-FRIED TROUT WITH FRESH SAGE

*In this simple dish, wild sage from the hills is used for color
and to enhance the flavor of the trout. Pan-frying is a pleasurable way to
cook whole fish and ensures the fish retains its color and moisture.*

SERVES 4

| | |
|---|---|
| 4 whole trout, weighing about 8 ounces each, gutted and cleaned<br>Flour, seasoned<br>4 tablespoons butter | Handful of fresh sage leaves<br>¼ cup white wine<br>¼ cup brandy<br>Sea salt and freshly ground black pepper |

1 Dry the fish well with paper towels. Coat each trout with seasoned flour, shaking off the excess.

2 In a large, heavy pan, heat the butter and sage leaves over a high heat. When the butter has browned a little, take out the sage leaves and put aside. Add the trout and fry them for a couple of minutes on each side, turning only once, until both sides are golden and crisp.

3 Reduce the heat, then replace the sage leaves and pour in the wine and brandy. Cook gently for 4–5 minutes more on each side. Season and serve immediately.

*Coming in with the catch, in the late-afternoon sun, Grossetto.*

# Baccalà in Dolceforte

### SALT COD WITH RAISINS AND PINE NUTS

*Until recently, fresh fish was virtually unavailable in landlocked areas of Tuscany and so* baccalà, *cod preserved in salt, became a reliable staple for Fridays and Lenten dishes.* Baccalà *is still a much-loved delicacy in many parts of Tuscany.*

### SERVES 6

| | |
|---|---|
| 2 pounds salt cod | Sea salt and freshly ground |
| Flour | black pepper |
| Extra-virgin olive oil | ½ cup pine nuts |
| 3 garlic cloves, chopped | ½ cup raisins |
| 2 pounds tomatoes, peeled | A little chopped fresh parsley |
| and chopped | |

1 A day in advance, put the salt cod in a bowl in the sink, leaving the tap running slightly to ensure a constant change of water. Allow it to soak for 24 hours.

2 On the serving day, strip the skin off the cod, remove any bones, dry it and cut it into square pieces. Coat the pieces with flour and fry them in very hot olive oil, until they are brown on all sides. Drain on paper towels.

3 For the sauce, heat some more oil and brown the garlic. Add the tomatoes, seasoning, pine nuts, raisins and chopped parsley. Let the sauce simmer for 20 minutes.

4 Add the fish pieces to the sauce for a few minutes to warm through. Serve this dish with lightly cooked green beans or broccoli.

### Cook's Notes

*At its best, salt cod is deliciously creamy, but it does need to be soaked according to the method described above, to rehydrate it and remove the salt.*

P erhaps because meat has always symbolized abundance in Italy, vegetarianism has never really taken off. When a vegetarian friend recently in Tuscany expressed her preferences she was treated with sympathetic glances and comments like "*oh, che poverina!*" "poor thing"! And yet, with its abundance of crops around the year, Tuscany is a haven for vegetarians, or vegetable-lovers in general. Though their treatment is certainly not as imaginative as, say, in Naples or Sicily, the ingredients are of the highest quality. Vegetables make up a substantial part of each meal. First courses will use potatoes and *cavolo nero* – a type of long-leaf cabbage – for hearty soups, artichokes for pasta sauces or wild

# VEGETABLES

mushrooms for risottos. Rustic sauces for the second course are founded on a standard *base di cottura* – cooking base – of celery, carrot and onion, and no meal is complete without a *contorno*, or side dish of vegetables alone.

Soups have always played an important part in the peasant diet. The *cavolo nero* (black cabbage) soup mentioned earlier is perhaps the most important. Called *ribollita* in Florence, its name comes from the inclusion of leftover beans from an

earlier meal which are then "reboiled." *Zuppa di ceci* is chick-pea soup, popular in various guises all over the Mediterranean. In Lucca, the local soup, *garmucia*, is a combination of fava beans, artichokes, peas and asparagus tips. *Pappa al pomodoro* is a tasty soup from harder times: it is a porridge of stale bread, tomatoes and basil stewed in a bone broth until it is of rib-sticking heartiness.

A more delicate soup, found only in the Tuscan capital, is *cinestrata*, whose strange marriage of sweet and savory is said to be a Renaissance legacy from the days when Florence was the center of trade with the east. Its base of poultry and vegetable broth is heightened with Marsala, then thickened with egg. Just before serving it is sprinkled with sugar, cinnamon and nutmeg.

In Tuscany, seasonal crops are used in simple, delicious dishes around the year. In spring, country people gather young nettles, borage, dandelion and wild herbs to make nettle risotto (*risotto all'ortica*), vegetable soufflé (*sformato*) or simple herb salads (*insalata con erbe aromatiche*).

If the artichoke reigns supreme in Rome, spinach is king in Tuscany. The abundant crop is the basis for *uova alla Fiorentina*, Florentine eggs on a bed of spinach. Its peculiar metallic aftertaste is found in *risotta verde* and in *gnocchi*. For while the Roman version of the latter is characteristically made with potatoes (*see* Bread, Beans and Pasta), and those of Piedmont and Liguria with semolina, the classic gnocchi of Tuscany are a marriage of ricotta cheese, spinach and flour. Rather confusingly, they are known locally as *ravioli di spinaci*; ravioli here is used in the old Tuscan sense of a dumpling. If the recipe uses no flour as a binding agent, it is sometimes known as *malfatti* ("badly made"). When a menu offers *ravioli con spinaci*, however, you can expect the little stuffed pillows we all know and love.

Spinach is also the star of *torta di spinaci*, a tart incorporating cheese and eggs or, more elaborately, ricotta, peas and chokeless baby artichokes. If presented as a side dish, spinach is often steamed and then tossed lightly with olive oil, lemon and garlic juice (*spinaci in padella*).

Asparagus appears in the markets in the spring. The long, thin shoots are cooked *al dente* and then served alone or with *prosciutto*, or chopped into a thick *frittata* omelet, or stuffed into crêpes. Crisp white fennel, with its fresh aniseed flavor, is eaten with *mentuccia* (wild mint). *Risotta alla paesana* (country-style risotto) combines many of the choicest young springtime vegetables – new celery and carrots, early peas and zucchini – with bacon, tomatoes, Parmesan and, of course, rice.

Summer's shiny and firm zucchini are sautéed and added to omelets and *sformato*. Their saffron-colored flowers (*fiori di zucchini*) are stuffed with ham and mozzarella, dipped into batter and fried. At the end of the season, ripe plum tomatoes and enormous bunches of fragrant basil are piled up in the markets. *Panzanella* salad, using bread, tomatoes, basil, capers and olive oil, appears on Tuscan country tables and rich, red sauces are served with fresh pasta and boiled *cannellini* beans. Dusky eggplants, sliced thinly, grilled over the open fire and drizzled with olive oil, are eaten as starters and side dishes.

### FRUITS OF THE FOREST

By autumn, it is time to gather wild mushrooms – *porcini* (ceps) and chanterelles – from the chestnut, oak and pine

POLENTA – THE GOLD OF THE NORTH

While Italian Americans have been responsible for many "typically American" dishes – pizza, the meatball "grinder" sandwich, and tomato ketchup among them – polenta resulted from a gift of the New World to the Old. With the explorers returning from the Americas came corn; soon it was being cultivated in northern Italy and its dried kernels ground to make a pale yellow, grainy flour. Stirred with water slowly over the fire, this *polenta* made a heavy pudding, which could either be eaten immediately as a soft mush, or allowed to cool into a hard cake or loaf, which could be cut into

slices and fried or grilled. It became a staple of the Veneto, Lombardy and Tuscany and, in the case of the poor, largely supplanted bread.

In the Tuscan tradition, either form is usually served with a moistening meat sauce or a bean and cabbage stew. Alternatively, the polenta is stirred directly into vegetable soup to make a hearty meal. One version, *infarinata* ("grain mixed in"), a speciality of Garfagnana, is a creamy mixture of the polenta, *cannellini* beans, *cavalo nero* (long-leaved "black" cabbage) and *pancetta* (smoked and salted bacon).

forests. Mushrooms, like chestnuts, form an integral part of the *cucina povera* since they were always a staple to the very poor. Sautéed with garlic they accompany *pisci*, the home-made stringy pasta, or are stewed *in umido* as the base for a thick soup. Some will be laid out to dry (*porcini secchi*) so that they can be enjoyed during the rest of the year. The largest *porcini* are studded with slivers of garlic and wild mint and simply grilled over the open fire. *Ovuli* mushrooms – rarer and with a more delicate flavor – are marinated in olive oil and lemon juice and eaten with Parmesan shavings.

November is truffle time, *la stagione del tartufo*. In the small area around Monte Amiata, the hunters set out to the oak forests with their trained dogs or pigs, whose sensitive noses are employed to sniff out the precious tubers. Any of the prize black truffles found will be used immediately, simply grated on to omelet, tagliatelle or fettucine or added to *porcini* to eke them out a little. Truffles are rare – no one has yet found a way of cultivating them – and therefore extremely expensive. For cooking, a good alternative is truffle paste – *crema di tartufi* – usually made up of truffles and *porcini*. This is sold in Italian stores.

Olives and walnuts and other familiar ingredients piled up at Florence's Mercato Centrale.

# Zuppa di Funghi Porcini

## WILD MUSHROOM SOUP

*In autumn, wild mushrooms are gathered from the woods of
the Maremma and brought home in large basketfuls. This richly flavored
soup is made with the most interesting varieties found.*

Chestnuts and porcini mushrooms are two of the highlights of the
autumn harvest.

## Cook's Notes

When wild mushrooms are not in season, you could
use some porcini secchi (dried porcini mushrooms),
pre-soaked for a couple of hours in warm water.

### SERVES 6

4 garlic cloves, chopped
Extra-virgin olive oil
2 pounds mixed wild and
cultivated mushrooms, wiped
and coarsely chopped
Large handful of finely
chopped fresh parsley
Large pinch of chili powder

Sea salt and freshly ground
black pepper
⅔ cup dry white wine
1 tablespoon tomato paste
2½ cups boiling water
6 thick slices of coarse white
bread, such as *ciabatta*

1 In a large, heavy pan, gently fry the garlic in the olive oil. Remove and reserve it.

2 Add more olive oil to the pan and, over a high flame, brown the mushrooms. Reduce the heat and replace the garlic. Add most of the parsley (save a little to garnish), the chili powder and seasoning. Cover the pan and cook over a medium heat, stirring occasionally, for 20 minutes.

3 Pour in the white wine and let the mixture bubble to evaporate the liquid, then add the tomato paste mixed with the boiling water. Bring to a boil, cover the pan, reduce the heat and simmer for 20 minutes more.

4 Grill the bread on both sides until it is very brown. Drizzle with more olive oil and place a slice in each soup bowl. Spoon over the mushroom soup. Garnish with the remaining chopped parsley and a drizzle of olive oil.

# RISOTTO VERDE

### GREEN RISOTTO

*This creamy risotto is from Enrico's restaurant, the* Antica Trattoria
*in Colle di Val d'Elsa. It makes an excellent first course for a fish meal. To achieve
the right consistency, use arborio rice, which has a sticky texture.*

### SERVES 4

2 onions, finely sliced
4 tablespoons butter
12 ounces arborio rice
⅔ cup dry white wine
3 cups chicken or fish stock
⅔ cup light cream
1 pound spinach, cooked,
drained and finely chopped

½ cup fresh parsley, chopped
4 ounces cooked ham,
finely chopped
4 ounces Parmesan cheese,
grated
Sea salt and freshly ground
black pepper

1 Cook the onions in some of the butter over a gentle heat for a few minutes until they are soft.

2 Stir in the rice, add the remaining butter and cook for a few minutes over a higher heat, stirring, until the rice starts to crackle. Reduce the heat a little and then add the wine and stir for a couple of minutes. Add the warmed stock a ladleful at a time, stirring all the time, and waiting for each lot to be absorbed before adding the next. Finally, add the cream.

3 Stir in the spinach, parsley, ham, half the Parmesan, a little salt (not too much because the ham and Parmesan are salty) and some pepper. Cook for a further 20 minutes or so, stirring every so often. The risotto should be creamy in texture and the rice just *al dente*. Serve warm, topped with the remaining Parmesan cheese.

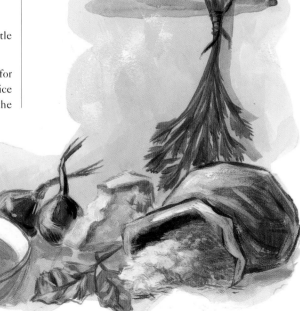

# RISOTTO AL POMODORO

## TOMATO RISOTTO WITH BASIL AND HOME-DRIED TOMATOES

*This risotto, a slight departure from Tuscan tradition, is nevertheless*
*Tuscan-inspired in its respect for simple, well blended flavors. The intense flavor*
*of the tomatoes works well with the creaminess of the risotto and the basil.*

### SERVES 4

FOR THE HOME-DRIED
TOMATOES
Extra-virgin olive oil
Balsamic vinegar
Sea salt and freshly ground
black pepper
Large pinch of sugar
8–10 medium plum
tomatoes, halved lengthways

FOR THE RISOTTO
1 medium onion, finely
chopped
2 carrots, finely chopped
1 celery stalk, finely chopped
Extra-virgin olive oil
13 ounces plum tomatoes,
skinned and chopped, or
canned tomatoes, chopped,
with their juice

2 tablespoons tomato purée
1 teaspoon sugar
Sea salt and freshly ground
black pepper
12 ounces arborio rice
4 tablespoons butter
⅔ cup red or white wine
3 cups good hot vegetable
stock
⅔ cup light cream
4 ounces Parmesan cheese,
grated, plus more for serving
Large handful of fresh basil
leaves, torn

1 Start the home-dried tomatoes the night before you are to make the risotto. Mix together some olive oil, balsamic vinegar, salt, pepper and a large pinch of sugar and brush this dressing over the halved tomatoes. Place in the oven at the very lowest setting and leave overnight to dry out.

2 For the risotto sauce, gently fry the onion, carrot and celery in olive oil until the onion is transparent. Add the chopped tomatoes, their juice, tomato purée, sugar, salt and pepper. Bring to the boil, reduce the heat and simmer for 30 minutes.

3 Meanwhile, fry the rice in the butter until it starts to crackle. Add the wine and cook for about two minutes. Add the warmed stock little by little, stirring all the time and waiting for it to be absorbed before adding the next.

4 Stir in the tomato sauce, cream and grated Parmesan and continue to cook, still stirring, until the rice is *al dente*. Finally, stir in the torn basil leaves.

5 Serve each portion piled with home-dried tomatoes and Parmesan shavings.

# MALFATTI

### SPINACH AND RICOTTA DUMPLINGS

Malfatti, *"badly made,"* literally, apparently take their name from
the fact that they appear to be a pasta dish but in fact do not contain pasta.
*This makes a warming winter's dish.*

### SERVES 4

| | |
|---|---|
| 2 pounds spinach | FOR THE WHITE SAUCE |
| 1 pound ricotta cheese | 2 tablespoons butter |
| 1 egg, beaten | 3 tablespoons flour |
| ½ teaspoon freshly | 1¼ cups milk |
| grated nutmeg | Large pinch of freshly |
| Sea salt and freshly ground | grated nutmeg |
| black pepper | Sea salt and freshly ground |
| 4 ounces Parmesan cheese, | black pepper |
| grated | |

*An ancient Elban farmhouse nestles in the shade of trees.*

1 Preheat the oven to 500°F. Wash the spinach well and cook it over a gentle heat in only the water that clings to the leaves. Drain well, chop finely and mix with the ricotta, beaten egg, nutmeg, salt, pepper and half the Parmesan.

2 For the sauce, melt the butter in a heavy pan and cook with the flour for 1 minute, stirring continuously. Take the pan off the heat and add the milk gradually, stirring all the time. Bring the mixture to the boil and continue to stir until the mixture thickens. Off the heat, stir in the nutmeg and seasoning.

3 Grease a shallow dish and pour in half the sauce. With wet hands, make the spinach and ricotta mixture into dumplings and place these in the dish.

4 Top with the rest of the sauce, the remaining Parmesan and some more freshly ground black pepper.

5 Bake at the top of the oven for 8–10 minutes, or until the cheese is brown and bubbling. Serve immediately.

# Finocchi all'Aglio e Prezzemolo

## Sautéed Fennel with Garlic and Parsley

*Sautéed fennel has a subtle flavor that makes it a good
accompaniment for fish. It should be very pale in color and tightly packed..
The green shoots can be chopped finely and used to garnish the dish.*

### Serves 4

| | |
|---|---|
| 4 small, crisp fennel bulbs | Sea salt and freshly ground |
| Lemon juice | black pepper |
| Extra-virgin olive oil | Small handful of fresh |
| 3 garlic cloves, unpeeled | parsley or mint, chopped |

1 Trim the fennel and cut into quarters from top to base, so that each piece remains intact.

2 Boil in water with a little lemon juice for 5 minutes; drain and pat dry.

3 Heat some olive oil in a wide, heavy pan and fry the unpeeled garlic cloves for a couple of minutes. Remove the cloves with a slotted spoon and discard them.

4 Brown the fennel on both sides and season it, then reduce the heat and sauté until the pieces are tender (about 10 minutes).

5 A minute before serving, stir in the chopped parsley or mint. Serve immediately.

*A quiet street in Sorano, during the siesta-hour; open shutters let in cooling breezes.*

# CRESPELLE AGLI ASPARAGI

## ASPARAGUS-STUFFED CREPES

*This recipe, from* Ristorante Al Marsili *in Siena, is perfect for the spring, when the first young asparagus shoots appear in the markets. With its light asparagus and cream sauce filling it makes a good first course for an elegant dinner.*

### SERVES 4

FOR THE CREPES
1 egg, beaten
⅔ cup milk
⅔ cup water
1 cup flour
Sea salt and freshly ground
black pepper
Vegetable oil

FOR THE FILLING
1 pound asparagus
Extra-virgin olive oil
1 large garlic clove, chopped

Small bunch of fresh
parsley, chopped

FOR THE WHITE SAUCE
2 tablespoons butter
3 tablespoons flour
1¼ cups milk
1 ounce Parmesan
cheese, grated
Large pinch of freshly
grated nutmeg
Sea salt and freshly ground
black pepper

1 Make the crêpe batter by whisking together the beaten egg, milk, water, flour and seasoning. Refrigerate for 1 hour. Preheat the oven to 400°F.

2 Trim and wash the asparagus and cook it in boiling, salted water until it is *al dente*. Heat a little oil in a frying pan and brown the chopped garlic. Stir in the parsley. Roughly chop the asparagus and stir it in; continue frying for 2–3 minutes. Purée all in a blender or food processor.

3 For the sauce, melt the butter in a heavy pan and cook it with the flour for a minute, stirring continuously. Remove the pan from the heat and add the milk gradually, stirring all the time. Bring the mixture to the boil and continue to stir until the mixture thickens. Off the heat, stir in the Parmesan, nutmeg, seasoning and the asparagus mixture.

4 Fry the crêpes in a small, heavy pan over a very high heat. If you are not filling them immediately, layer them on a plate, placing a sheet of wax paper between each crêpe to keep them separate.

5 Put a spoonful of the asparagus filling onto each crêpe and roll, tucking in the ends to form packages. Reserve some stuffing to pour over the top. Place the filled crêpes on a greased baking tray and pour over the remaining filling. Cook at the top of the oven for 15–20 minutes. Serve hot.

## Cook's Notes

These pancakes are also very good with young artichokes. Parboil the hearts for 5 minutes, drain, pat dry and sauté them in olive oil with garlic, then liquidize them and add to a béchamel sauce in the same way.

# CIPOLLINE IN AGRODOLCE

## ONIONS IN SWEET AND SOUR SAUCE WITH GRAPES

*The sweet–savory flavors of this Renaissance dish
make it a good accompaniment to game. Small, mild onions can
be found in Italian grocers or larger supermarkets.*

### SERVES 4

| | |
|---|---|
| 2 tablespoons sugar | Sea salt and freshly ground |
| 2 tablespoons butter | black pepper |
| 1 pound small Italian onions, | 3 ounces black grapes, halved |
| peeled | and seeded |
| ¼ cup white wine | |

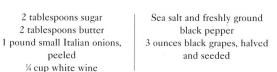

1 Heat the sugar in a heavy pan with a tablespoon of water until it caramelizes. Immediately stir in the butter.

2 Toss the onions in the mixture for a couple of minutes, then pour in the wine. Season, bring to a boil, cover, reduce the heat and simmer for 20 minutes.

3 Add the grapes and simmer for 10 minutes more, uncovered, to reduce the liquid. Adjust the seasoning before serving.

# ERBE SALTATE IN PADELLA

SAUTÉED LEAF VEGETABLES

*This dish has a vibrant color and a delicate texture
that goes very well with fish. It's important not to overcook leaf
vegetables as they lose their color and become limp.*

SERVES 4

2 pounds mixed leaf
vegetables, such as spinach,
beet greens or chard
Good olive oil
Sea salt and freshly ground
black pepper

Pinch of freshly
grated nutmeg
Lemon juice

1 Wash the leaves well and cook them gently for 4–5 minutes, in only the water that clings to them.

2 Drain the leaves. (Do not chop them because this will ruin the texture.)

3 Sauté the leaves very gently in some olive oil for 2–3 minutes. Add seasoning and nutmeg. Just before serving, sprinkle with a little lemon juice.

Market day in Colle di Val d'Elsa, and the array of produce is dazzling.

# Patate al Forno

ROASTED POTATOES WITH ROSEMARY AND GARLIC

*These crunchy, herby potatoes make an excellent
accompaniment to roasted chicken or lamb. Waxy yellow potatoes and very
fresh rosemary and garlic will give the best results.*

SERVES 6–8

3 pounds waxy
yellow potatoes
3 garlic cloves,
finely chopped
Leaves of 1 sprig of
rosemary, chopped

Coarse sea salt and freshly
ground black pepper
4 tablespoons butter,
softened with a fork
¼ cup olive oil

1 Preheat the oven to 500°F. Peel or scrub the potatoes and cut each lengthwise into 4–6 wedges. Pat the pieces dry.

2 Pound the chopped garlic with the rosemary and lots of seasoning and mix in the butter and olive oil.

3 Rub this mixture all over the potatoes. Pack them into a roasting pan.

4 Cook at the top of the oven for an hour, basting occasionally, until the potatoes are very brown and crisp.

Early morning by an ancient fountain in the Piazza Grande, Montepulciano.

# POLENTA ALLA GRIGLIA

### GRILLED POLENTA

*Polenta is traditionally eaten in the winter with rich game stews. Many recipes call for it to be deep-fried, but it is just as good brushed with olive oil and broiled, or grilled on a griddle if you have one, until it is crisp and brown.*

### SERVES 4

| | |
|---|---|
| 3 cups water | Extra-virgin olive oil |
| Salt | Freshly ground black pepper |
| 3 cups polenta | |

1 Bring the water to the boil in a large pan, with some salt. When the water is bubbling, add the polenta in a slow, steady stream, stirring continuously to prevent lumps from forming.

2 Lower the heat and simmer, stirring at very regular intervals, for about 20 minutes or until the polenta starts coming away from the sides of the pan.

3 Pour into a loaf pan or deep dish and allow to set.

4 Unmold the polenta and cut it into thick slices. Drizzle with olive oil, salt and freshly ground black pepper. Cook the slices under a hot broiler until they are crisp and golden on both sides.

# Sformato di Zucchini

## Zucchini Mousse

*A* sformato *(literally meaning "unmolded") is a cross between a soufflé and an egg custard. Diva, at the* Trattoria Diva e Maceo *in Montepulciano, serves* sformato *as an accompaniment to beef or lamb cooked over charcoal.*

### Serves 6

1½ pounds small, firm zucchini, finely sliced
Extra-virgin olive oil
2 tablespoons butter
3 tablespoons flour
1¼ cups milk
Large pinch of freshly grated nutmeg

3 ounces Parmesan cheese, grated
Sea salt and freshly ground black pepper
3 eggs, separated
1½ cups fresh white bread crumbs

1 Preheat the oven to 400°F. Fry the zucchini gently in olive oil for 4–5 minutes, or until they are soft and slightly golden.

2 For the sauce, cook the butter and flour in a small, heavy pan for a minute, stirring all the time. Remove from the heat and add the milk gradually. Bring to a boil, stirring continuously, until the sauce thickens.

3 Off the heat, add the nutmeg, half the grated Parmesan, the egg yolks and salt and pepper. Stir in the fried zucchini slices.

4 Beat the egg whites until they are stiff, and carefully fold them into the cooled sauce.

5 Mix the remaining Parmesan with the bread crumbs and line a well greased dish with half of the mixture. Pour the *sformato* into the dish and top with the remaining Parmesan and bread crumbs.

6 Bake in the middle of the oven for 35 minutes, or until the mixture has set and the top is golden brown. Unmold and serve immediately.

# Insalata con Erbe Aromatiche

## GREEN SALAD WITH WILD HERBS

*This fragrant salad makes an excellent accompaniment to
any meat dish. Use as wide a variety of leaves and fresh herbs as possible –
the more flavors, the more interesting the salad will be.*

### SERVES 4

2 Bibb lettuces, or 1 head of
romaine
Inner leaves of 1 radicchio,
or some chicory leaves
Handful of arugula leaves
Small handfuls of
fresh chives, mint, basil,
tarragon and dill
1 fennel bulb, thinly sliced

FOR THE DRESSING
Cloudy extra-virgin olive oil
Few drops of balsamic
vinegar or sweet
red-wine vinegar
Sea salt and freshly
ground black pepper

Fresh, aromatic Tuscan herbs, including sage and rosemary, in
the mercato centrale, Florence.

1 Wash and pat dry all the salad leaves. Wash, dry and
chop the herbs. Mix everything together and toss in the
fennel slices.

2 Mix the dressing ingredients together.

3 To preserve the crispness of the leaves, dress the salad
immediately before serving, or put the oil, vinegar, salt
and pepper on the table for people to dress their own.

## Cook's Notes

For this salad, use the very best cloudy (unfiltered)
olive oil you can find.

Tuscany does not produce much cheese, but its sheep's-milk cheese, *pecorino*, whose name comes from *pecora*, meaning sheep, is renowned as excellent. The handsome little Renaissance town of Pienza, in the gentle hills of the Val d'Orcia, is justly famous for its *pecorino*. Here, sheep have grazed for centuries on the herbs of the nearby *Crete Senese*, giving the cheese its distinctive, aromatic flavor. Pienza hosts a *pecorino* fair on the first Sunday of September, when the cheeses from the surrounding farms can be tasted. As the day fades,

# DAIRY PRODUCTS, FRUIT AND NUTS

people settle in the town's square to watch a game of *cacio al fuso*, "roll-the-cheese," in which participants have to roll a wheel of cheese into a target.

*Pecorino* is eaten in various stages of maturity. There is the soft, creamy, weeks-old *pecorino fresco* and the medium mature *pecorino rosso*. Its red rind was traditionally made from sheep's blood; now, this comes from tomato paste. The strongest is *pecorino stagionato*, a few months old and with a rich and sweet flavor. In villages, tiny shops display extremely mature, yellow *pecorino*, with signs proudly proclaiming "five months old and never been in the refrigerator!".

Making *pecorino* is an art. The milk is gently heated with a coagulant – traditionally, wild artichoke – stirred, and then left to stand until it has the consistency of stiff yogurt. It is poured into molds and squeezed countless times to separate the curds from the whey. The milky whey that runs out of the cheese is re-boiled to make light ricotta, literally, "recooked" cheese. Usually mixed with spinach for fresh pasta stuffings and to make cheesecakes, this ricotta is also delicious with honey, mint or freshly ground coffee and sugar. The curds are left to set on wooden shelves and turned regularly.

some of the best trattorie lie behind siena's magnificent Palazzo Pubblico.

## FRUIT

Fruit is an integral part of every Italian meal. No matter how many courses have been eaten, the meal will always end with two or three large dishes of seasonal fruit placed in the middle of the table. A leisurely lunch or dinner is thus prolonged, and conversation continues as fruit is pensively peeled and nuts are cracked.

Tuscany has good fruit. In spring, street-market stalls are piled high with dark, shiny cherries. In summer, there are wild strawberries, juicy peaches, apricots, sweet melons and scarlet water-melons. By autumn, figs, grapes, wild quinces and juicy persimmons appear. In winter, the stalls are full of little oranges and blood oranges from Sicily. Desserts other than fruit are usually reserved for Sundays and holidays. In

Tuscany, these tend to be fairly simple: nutty *cantuccini* to dunk in *vin santo*; a seasonal fruit tart, *crostata*, or *semifreddo* or *zuccotto*, which are types of ice cream with cake, fruit and mascarpone cream. The justly famous ice creams and sorbets of Florence are eaten as part of the ritual of the summer evening stroll or *passeggiata*.

### Nuts

Many of Tuscany's sweetmeats, made with local chestnuts, eggs, nuts and honey, are linked to the culinary heritage of the religious orders. In the Middle Ages, convents played an important role in the life of the town, accommodating both guests from out of town and ministering to the poor. With the honey, eggs and nuts from their own land, the nuns created little cookies for the numerous saints' days throughout the year. Some of these have quite odd names. *Ossi dei morti* ("dead man's bones") commemorate the Day of the Dead (November 1st). Made from egg white and crystallized sugar, they crack and crunch, supposedly like bones, when bitten into. Uneven piled hazelnut cookies are called *brutti ma buoni*, "ugly but good." There is *dolce del diavolo*, "the Devil's cake," with chocolate and cinnamon as the tempter, and *pane coi Santi*, "bread of the Saints," with walnuts, pine nuts and figs, made on All Saints' Day.

Nuts have different historical associations too. Almonds have had an elevated status since ancient times. In Asian mythology, the almond tree, perhaps because it blossomed first, was considered the father of the world. In Tuscany, almonds are associated with special occasions, to make *ricciarelli* (soft almond-paste biscuits) and *panforte*, the medieval sweetmeat packed with whole almonds.

Chestnuts, by contrast, as the historic staple for the very poor, have always had humbler associations. At the end of the year they are made into thick, nourishing soups and roasted over the fire's embers. The chestnuts are ground down for flour (*farina di castagne*) to make *castagnaccio*. This flat, dense cake with raisins, pine nuts and rosemary, originally a speciality of Lucca, is sometimes called "the panforte of the poor." It's rather dull: Tuscans insist that it is an acquired taste! Fresh walnuts are associated with Christmas and festivities, eaten on their own or on walnut cake, *torta di noce*. In Siena, little *cavallucci* biscuits combine fresh walnuts with orange, candied peel, aniseed and spices.

# PECORINO E PERE

## PECORINO AND PEARS

*The classic marriage of pear and mature sheep's-milk cheese is immortalized in the old Tuscan saying, "Al contadino non far sapere quanto e buono il pecorino con le pere" ("you don't need to tell a peasant that pecorino goes with pears").*

**SERVES 4**

12 ounces *pecorino stagionato*
4 ripe autumn pears

1 Place the whole pears in the middle of a cheese board.

2 Arrange the cheese, cut into very thin slices, around the edges.

## Cook's Notes

soft, mild pecorino fresco goes very well with ripe strawberries sprinkled with lemon juice, purple figs or grapes.

A Tuscan shepherd samples the pecorino yield, with local bread.

# PESCHE RIPIENE

### STUFFED PEACHES

*Make this dessert with summer's juicy yellow peaches and serve it hot with cold whipped cream or* crema di mascarpone *(see page 83). The huge yellow peaches seen in Italian markets are ideal, but smaller, ripe red peaches will do also.*

### SERVES 4

4 ripe yellow peaches, halved
and stoned
2 ounces Amaretti biscuits
(bitter macaroons), crushed
¼ cup Amaretto liqueur or
Marsala
1 large egg yolk
2 tablespoons sugar
3 tablespoons cocoa powder
2 tablespoons butter
Juice of 1 lemon

1 Preheat the oven to 350°F. Scoop out a little of the flesh from the center of each peach half and mash the pulp with the crushed macaroons, liqueur, egg yolk, sugar and cocoa powder.

2 Fill the peach hollows with the stuffing and arrange them on a greased baking tray. On each peach half, put small pieces of butter, a little lemon juice and a sprinkling of sugar.

3 Bake for 30 minutes, or until the peaches are golden. Serve hot.

# TORTA DI NOCE

## WALNUT TART

*This delicious tart was created one December at the*
Ristorante Il Prato *in Pienza to celebrate the walnut harvest. Fiorella serves*
*the torta with* vin santo, *the famous amber dessert wine of the region.*

### SERVES 8–10

2¾ cups flour
4 large egg yolks
1¼ cups sugar
8 ounces (2 sticks) butter

8 ounces walnut halves
½ cup apricot jam
Confectioners' sugar, to dust

1 Cut the butter into the flour. Mix in the sugar and then add the egg yolks and mix with your hands, to form a moist crumbly dough. Wrap in plastic wrap and refrigerate for 2 hours. Allow the dough to stand for about an hour to readjust to room temperature before rolling it out.

2 Preheat the oven to 375°F and toast the walnut halves on a baking tray in the oven.

3 Divide the dough into two. Place half the dough between two sheets of floured plastic wrap and shape it into a square with the tips of your fingers. Continue to roll it in this shape, using quick, light movements. Roll the second half to the same size.

4 Slip one half of the pastry onto a rectangular baking tray approximately 16 × 12 inches, using the plastic wrap to help you.

5 Spread with a thick layer of apricot jam. Roughly chop half of the walnuts and sprinkle them on top. Cover this layer with the second sheet of pastry.

6 Bake in the middle of the oven for 30 minutes, or until the top is golden brown.

7 Remove from the oven and reduce the heat to 325°F. Push the remaining walnut halves evenly on to the pastry. Put the tart back into the oven for a further 10 minutes. Cut into squares and serve cold, dusted with confectioners' sugar.

# TORTA DI RICOTTA

## RICOTTA TART

*Ricotta (meaning "recooked") is the reboiled whey of milk after the curds have been separated to make cheese. Tuscan ricotta, usually from sheep's milk, arrives each morning from neighbouring farms to the village* alimentari, *still warm and wobbly.*

### SERVES 6

| FOR THE PASTRY | FOR THE FILLING |
|---|---|
| 2⅓ cups flour | ½ cup pine nuts |
| ½ teaspoon baking powder | 6 tablespoons grappa or rum |
| 7 tablespoons sugar | ½ cup raisins |
| 1½ sticks cold | 1 pound ricotta cheese |
| butter, cubed | 2 large eggs |
| 2 large egg yolks | ½ cup sugar |
| | Zest of 3 lemons |

1 For the pastry, mix the flour, baking powder and sugar and sift them together. Cut in the butter and then mix in the egg yolks to form a firm dough. Wrap loosely and chill for 45 minutes.

2 Preheat the oven to 400°F and toast the pine nuts on a baking tray in the oven until golden. Soak the raisins in the grappa or rum.

3 Push the ricotta through a food mill or a wire strainer into a large mixing bowl (this process incorporates air). Mix in the eggs, toasted pine nuts, grappa- or rum-soaked raisins and their soaking liquid, sugar and lemon zest.

4 Divide the pastry in half and roll out one piece to line a 10-inch tart pan. Fill the tart shell with the ricotta mixture. Roll the remaining pastry for the top. Seal the edges with wet fingers. Brush the top with beaten egg and score it with a knife.

5 Bake for 40 minutes, or until the top is crisp and golden. Serve cold.

*Passing the time of day in the noonday heat, Monteriggioni.*

## Cook's Notes

Ricotta sold loose by weight tends to be lighter and contain fewer additives than pre-packed ricotta. It is available from most Italian delicatessens. Ricotta tart is best eaten fresh – preferably on the day it is made.

# MONT BLANC

## CHESTNUT MOUSSE

*Wild chestnuts picked between October and December
are eaten at Christmas in this soft mounded mousse, topped with whipped cream
and, to be really extravagant,* marrons glacés.

### SERVES 4

| | |
|---|---|
| 1 pound chestnuts | ½ teaspoon vanilla extract |
| 1¾ cups whipping cream | ⅔ cup hazelnuts, halved and |
| ¾ cup sugar, | toasted, or 2 *marrons glacés* |
| or to taste | (candied chestnuts), halved, |
| 6 tablespoons rum | to decorate |

The rich red and golden colours of chestnut woods in late autumn, Arezzo.

1 Score the top of the chestnuts and blanch them in boiling water for 15 minutes. Drain them and peel them when they are cool enough to handle. Bring them back to the boil and simmer for 1 hour, or until tender (this will depend on the age of the chestnuts).

2 Purée the chestnuts using a food mill, a blender or an electric mixer. Stir in half the cream and the sugar, together with the rum and the vanilla extract.

3 Cook over a gentle heat for five minutes, until the liquid has evaporated. Allow to cool. Whip the rest of the cream, with a little sugar if you like.

4 Mound the mousse onto serving plates with a dollop of cream on top. Scatter over the toasted hazelnuts or *marrons glacés*.

### Cook's Notes

When chestnuts are not in season (or if you feel like cheating) you could make this mousse successfully using canned, sweetened chestnut purée; you would need to omit the sugar and vanilla essence since these are already added to the purée.

# Cantuccini con Vin Santo e Crema di Mascarpone

## CANTUCCINI COOKIES WITH VIN SANTO AND MASCARPONE CREAM

*Cantuccini and small glasses of* vin santo *for dunking, served with big bowls of seasonal fruit, make a classic finish to a Tuscan dinner.*

### SERVES 5–6

| FOR THE COOKIES | FOR THE MASCARPONE CREAM |
|---|---|
| 1¾ cups whole unskinned almonds | 8 ounces mascarpone cheese |
| 3½ cups flour | 2 large egg yolks |
| 1 teaspoon baking powder | 4–5 tablespoons sugar |
| 1¼ cups sugar | ¼ cup Cointreau or Grand Marnier |
| 4 large eggs, roughly beaten | *vin santo*, to serve |
| 4–5 drops of vanilla extract | |
| Zest of 2 lemons | |

1 Preheat the oven to 400°F and toast the almonds on a baking sheet until golden.

2 For the cookies, sift the flour, baking powder and sugar into a large bowl and make a well in the middle.

3 Add the beaten eggs, vanilla extract, lemon zest and nuts (if you are using a mixer, add the nuts at the last minute so as not to break them) and work into a dough.

4 Roll the dough into long strips about 2 inches wide. Place on a greased, floured baking tray and bake for 15 minutes.

5 Cut the cookies at an angle into slices ¾ inch wide, and return them to the oven for 10 minutes more, or until they are golden brown. (You should have about 40 cookies).

6 For the mascarpone cream, mix the mascarpone, egg yolks, sugar and Cointreau or Grand Marnier to a smooth cream. Serve cold, with the cookies, dunking them alternately into the glasses of *vin santo* and small bowls of mascarpone cream.

# TORTINE DI RISO

### CREAMY RICE TARTLETS

*This is a classic tea-time cake, seen in* pasticcerie *in Florence and Lucca, with dainty little wrappers. It's a delicate, creamy rice and custard filling encased in short, crisp pastry.*

### SERVES 5–6

FOR THE PASTRY
1½ cups flour, sifted
⅓ cup sugar
6 tablespoons unsalted butter
1 large egg yolk

FOR THE FILLING
⅔ cup arborio or short-grain
rice

2½ cups water
5 large egg yolks
⅔ cup sugar
½ cup flour, sifted
2 cups milk
1 tablespoon butter
4–5 drops of vanilla extract
6 tablespoons rum
Confectioners' sugar, to serve

1 For the pastry, sift together the flour and sugar and cut in the butter. Add the egg yolk and a little very cold water and quickly mix to a firm dough. Wrap loosely and chill for 30 minutes.

2 Preheat the oven to 400°F. Cook the rice in the water for 35–40 minutes, or until completely tender and cooked through.

3 For the filling, beat the egg yolks and sugar with an electric mixer for 2–3 minutes, or until they are thick and pale. Beat in the flour. Heat the milk to boiling point and beat it into the egg mixture, with the mixer on its lowest setting, in a thin stream of drops.

4 Heat this custard, stirring with a wire whisk, until it thickens (it will be lumpy at first but will smooth out as you beat). Continue to cook over a low heat for a couple of minutes, to cook the flour.

5 Remove from the heat and beat in the butter, vanilla extract and rum. Stir in the cooked rice.

6 Grease a 10-inch tart pan, or individual tartlet molds. Roll out the pastry and use to line the pan(s). Pour in the filling. Bake for 35 minutes, or until the edges of the pastry and the top are golden brown. Serve cold, dusted with a little confectioners' sugar.

# Ricciarelli

## Sienese Almond Macaroons

*These soft, almondy cookies are the pride of Sienese cake shops, particularly
of the famous* Pasticceria Nannini *in the heart of the medieval city. The perfect*
ricciarello *is crisp and powdery on the outside and tender and moist on the inside.*

### Makes about 16 macaroons

| | |
|---|---|
| 1 cup whole blanched almonds, or 1¼ cups ground almonds | ⅛ teaspoon baking powder |
| 2 large egg whites | 1 cup confectioners' sugar, sifted, plus more for rolling and dusting |
| 2 tablespoons flour, sifted | 3–4 drops of almond extract |

1 Preheat the oven to 425°F and, if using whole almonds, toast the almonds on a baking tray until golden. Grind the almonds when they have cooled.

2 Beat the egg whites until they are stiff. Sift together the flour and baking powder and fold them into the egg whites. Fold in the confectioners' sugar, ground almonds and almond extract, to make a soft paste.

3 Pour confectioners' sugar onto the worktop and, for each cookie, roll a heaping teaspoonful of the paste in the icing sugar and then press it into an oblong shape, using the palm of your hand.

4 Place the cookies well apart from each other on a thoroughly greased baking tray. Bake for 10–12 minutes, or until the cookies are pale golden and slightly cracked and the inside is still soft.

5 When cold, dust with more confectioners' sugar.

*Nannini's, Siena, sells confectionery and cakes that are the stuff of dreams.*

# Panna Cotta con Frutti di Bosco

## "Cooked Cream" with Woodland Fruits

*The sharpness of woodland berries contrasts wonderfully
with this creamy mousse. Out of the berry season, accompany the
panna cotta with slices of ripe pear, plum or peach.*

The woods and valley around the ancient abbey of San'Antimo,
Montepulciano.

### Serves 4

1 small lemon
⅔ cup light cream
¼ cup sugar,
plus a little more
½ teaspoon vanilla extract
2 level teaspoons
powdered gelatin

2 tablespoons boiling water
⅔ cup whipping cream
2 cups mixed raspberries,
blueberries
and black currants

1 Peel off the lemon zest in a long strip and squeeze the juice. Heat the light cream with the sugar, vanilla extract and lemon zest until it comes to a boil (but do not let it actually boil or the cream will curdle). Dissolve the gelatin in the boiling water. Strain the cream mixture, then whisk in the gelatin and the lemon juice, reserving a tablespoon or so of juice for the fruit.

2 Whip the cream and fold in the cooled mixture.

3 Pour the *panna cotta* into small metal molds or into ramekins and chill for 3 hours.

4 An hour before serving, sprinkle the fruit with a little lemon juice and a little sugar.

5 To serve, turn the *panna cotta* out of their molds and spoon over the fruit.

# Zuccotto

MOLDED ICE CREAM CAKE

*This three-layered ice cream cake is called* zuccotto *because its unmolded form
resembles a halved pumpkin. It is usually made with a fatless sponge cake called*
pan di spagna *but* savoiardi *(ladyfingers) would do just as well.*

SERVES 5–6

½ cup hazelnuts, halved
6 tablespoons kirsch
2 tablespoons water
3 ounces sponge cake, sliced,
or *savoiardi* (ladyfingers)
1¼ cups whipping cream
3 tablespoons sugar
2–3 drops of vanilla extract
2 ounces whole preserved
(candied) fruit, chopped

2 ounces bittersweet
chocolate, plus more to
decorate
6 tablespoons rum or cognac
4 ounces ripe apricots or
strawberries, finely chopped
Cocoa powder, to decorate

1 Toast the hazelnuts in the oven on a baking tray, or in
a dry frying pan, until golden. Rub off any loose skins.
Dilute the kirsch with the water and dunk cake slices or
ladyfingers into it, then use them to line an 8-inch
diameter freezerproof bowl.

2 Whip one-third of the cream and fold in half of the
sugar, the chopped candied fruit and the vanilla
extract. Spread this mixture evenly over the cake
or ladyfingers and freeze for 20 minutes.

3 For the second layer, melt the chocolate
over a pan of hot water. Whip half of the
remaining cream. Fold in the chocolate,
with the toasted hazelnuts and rum or
cognac. Spread the chocolate cream evenly
over the first layer, using a metal spatula then
return the *zuccotto* to the freezer for 20
minutes.

4 For the third layer, whip the remaining cream and fold
in the remaining sugar and the chopped apricots or
strawberries. Fill the center with this and use up any
remaining cake or ladyfingers dunked in diluted kirsch for
the top. Return the *zuccotto* to the freezer for 3 hours.

5 Transfer the *zuccotto* to the refrigerator an hour before
serving. Unmold it and sprinkle some cocoa powder and
grated chocolate over the top and sides.

# Semifreddo al Grand Marnier

## GRAND MARNIER PARFAIT

*This elegant recipe makes the most of mascarpone's creaminess to create a simple, smooth ice cream. You can make the* **semifreddo** *well in advance and leave it in the freezer, but remember to take it out 45 minutes before serving to let it thaw a little.*

### SERVES 5

⅛ cup whole almonds
8 ounces mascarpone cheese
½ cup sugar
3 large eggs, separated

4 ounces bittersweet
chocolate
6 tablespoons Grand Marnier

1 Toast the almonds on a baking tray in the oven, or in a dry frying pan, until golden. When they are cool, roughly chop them.

2 Mix the mascarpone, sugar and egg yolks and stir in the chopped almonds.

3 Beat the egg whites to stiff peaks. Fold them into the mascarpone mixture, using a metal spoon. Pour into a tall glass bowl.

4 Melt the chocolate over a pan of just-boiling water and stir in the Grand Marnier. Spread with a metal spatula over the mascarpone mixture. Freeze for 3 hours.

5 Transfer the parfait from the freezer to the refrigerator 45 minutes before serving. Just before it goes to the table turn it out onto a flat plate.

# PANFORTE DI SIENA

### SIENESE SPICE CAKE

Panforte *dates from the fourteenth century, when the spice trade in Tuscany was starting to flourish. Traditionally made in December, it symbolized a prosperous and sweet New Year. It is still a much-loved sweet, served in thin slices with coffee after dinner.*

### SERVES 12

| | |
|---|---|
| 2 cups whole unskinned almonds | 3 tablespoons cocoa powder |
| ½ cup walnuts | 1¼ cups sugar |
| 1 cinnamon stick | 5 tablespoons clear honey |
| 1 tablespoon coriander seeds | 1 pound whole preserved |
| 6 cloves | (candied) fruit, chopped |
| 6 black peppercorns | 1 cup flour, sifted |
| 1 teaspoon freshly grated nutmeg | ½ cup sugar, sifted |

1 Preheat the oven to 350°F and toast the almonds and walnuts on a baking tray (keep them separate) until golden. Pound the cinnamon stick, walnuts, coriander seeds, cloves and peppercorns in a mortar and pestle. Stir in the nutmeg and cocoa powder.

2 Heat the sugar and honey in a saucepan, stirring continuously, until the mixture comes to a rolling boil. Continue to stir for half a minute, then remove from the heat and stir in the whole almonds, chopped candied fruit, walnut and cocoa mixture and sifted flour.

3 Pack the mixture into a round baking dish, flattening it with the back of a wooden spoon. Bake for 30 minutes.

4 Once the *panforte* has cooled, turn it out and dust it with sifted confectioners' sugar.

*Roofscape and architectural gems in an aerial view of Siena.*

# MENU PLANNER

*A family dinner for a Sunday or festive day consists of a first course* (primo) *of soup, fresh pasta or maybe risotto, a main course* (secondo) *of meat or fish with a side dish* (contorno) *of simply prepared vegetables, and a dessert* (dolce). *For non-festive days, meals tend to be less elaborate, say, a* primo *served with hunks of bread, a green salad or some seasonal vegetables, then fruit, then coffee. This menu-planning gazetteer will help you to decide on the best combinations for the occasion.*

## RENAISSANCE-STYLE DINNER

*Zuppa di ceci* 23
Chick-pea soup

*Faraona alla Medici* 40
Roast guinea fowl Medici-style

*Cinghiale in agrodolce* 46
Wild boar in sweet and sour sauce

*Cipolline in agrodolce* 68
Onions in sweet and sour sauce with grapes

*Panna cotta con frutti di bosco* 86
"Cooked cream" with woodland
(or other seasonal) fruits

*Panforte di Siena* 89
Sienese spice cake

WINE
*Brunello di Montalcino*

## SIENESE TRATTORIA-STYLE DINNER

*Ravioli con spinaci e ricotta* 31
Fresh ravioli with spinach and ricotta stuffing

*Sogliola al limone* 54
Fried sole with lemon

*Insalata mista*
Mixed leaf salad

*Cantuccini con Vin Santo e crema di mascarpone* 83
Cantuccini cookies with Vin Santo and
mascarpone cream

WINE
*Vernaccia di San Gimignano*

## SUMMER PICNIC UNDER THE TREES

*Pane di campagna* 15
Rustic country bread or *ciabatta*

*prosciutto e melone*
Prosciutto with melon

*Panzanella* 20
Summer salad

*Insalata mista*
Mixed leaf salad

*Finocchiona* 34
Fennel salame

*Pecorino e pere* 78
Pecorino and pears

*Torta di ricotta* 81
Ricotta tart

*Summer fruit* 76
Woodland strawberries, peaches, plums

WINE
*Vino da tavola*
Local table wine

## EASTER FAMILY LUNCH

*Crespelle agli asparagi* 00
Asparagus-stuffed crêpes

*Agnello arrosto* 47
Roast leg of spring lamb with rosemary and garlic

*Patate al forno* 70
Roasted potatoes with rosemary and garlic

*Finnochio all'aglio e prezzemolo* 66
Sautéed fennel with garlic and parsley

*Semifreddo al Grand Marnier* 88
Grand Marnier parfait

WINE
*Chianti Classico*

## LUNCH BY THE COAST

*Acciughe ripieni* 52
Stuffed fresh anchovies

*Linguine con seppie* 53
Linguine with squid and wine sauce

*Triglie grigliate* 54
Grilled red mullet with parsley and garlic stuffing

*Insalata con erbe aromatchie* 73
Green salad with wild herbs

Seasonal fruit

WINE
*vino da tavola*
White Tuscan table wine

### AFTERNOON TEA — *MERENDA* — IN FLORENCE

*Tortine di riso* 84
Creamy rice tartlets

*Torta di ricotta* 81
Ricotta tart

*Te o caffelatte*
Tea or milky coffee

### AUTUMNAL SUPPER

*Prosciutto crudo con fichi* 36
Prosciutto with purple figs

*Petti di pollo al tartufo e funghi porcini* 39
Chicken breasts with truffles and porcini mushrooms

*Erbe saltate in padella* 69
Sautéed leaf vegetables, platters of persimmons
and black grapes

*Cantuccini con Vin Santo e crema di mascarpone* 83
Cantuccini biscuits with Vin Santo wine
and mascarpone cream

WINE
A crisp white such as
*Vernaccia di San Gimignano*

### NEW YEAR'S EVE DINNER

*Crostini di fegatelli di pollo* 37
Chicken liver crostini

*Lenticchie e salsicce* 44
Sausages with brown lentils

*Insalata mista*
Mixed leaf salad

*Zuccotto* 87
Molded ice cream cake

*Panforte di Siena* 89
Sienese spice cake

WINE
*Rosso di Montalcino* or *Vino Nobile di Montepulciano*

# INDEX

# ACKNOWLEDGEMENTS

Quarto Publishing plc would like to thank the following for permission to reproduce copyright material: Stefano Caporali pp 8 & 9, F. Roiter/Image Bank p 10, Giuliano Colliva/Image Bank p 11, Vivienne Gonley p 13, Stefano Caporali pp 17 & 20, Michael Freeman p 22, AA Photo Library p 27, Ruth Corney p 29, Michael Freeman p 30, Vivienne Gonley p 35, Ruth Corney p 36, Lisl Dennis/Image Bank p 39, e.t.archive p 40, David Walsh p 43, John Grain p 44, Pictor p 47, Michael Freeman p 51, Andrea Pistolesi/Image Bank p 52, Michael Freeman p 56, Jay Freis/Image Bank p 61, David Walsh p 62, Andrea Pistolesi/Image Bank p 65, Pictor p 66, David Walsh p 69, Stefano Caporali pp 70 & 73, Pictor p 78, Maria Taglienti/Image Bank p 81, Stefano Caporali p 82, David Walsh p 85, John Grain p 86, P. Trummer/Image Bank p 89.
While every effort has been made to acknowledge all copyright holders, we apologize if any omissions have been made.